WHERE'S MY CASH?!

MY CASH?!

Testimony of a Money-Chaser

An in-the-trenches exposé of
accounts receivable management and why
it matters to your profit-seeking business

STU WOOLLEY

Library and Archives Canada Cataloguing
in Publication

Woolley, Stu, 1950-
Where's My Cash?! : Testimony of a life-long
professional money chaser / Stu Woolley. -- 1st Canadian ed.

ISBN 978-1-927375-00-6

1. Accounts receivable--Management. I. Title. II. Title:
Where's My Cash?!

HF5681.A3W66 2012   658.15'244   C2012-906492-0

IF
EVERYBODY
PAYS,
EVERYBODY
GETS PAID.

This book is dedicated to
my wife and advisor, Lesly

© STU WOOLLEY 2012

Hilborn:

PUBLISHED BY HILBORN GROUP INC.

ISBN#: 978-1-927375-00-6

Illustrations: Gail Barnhart-Anderson

Cover and complete book design:
John VanDuzer, WISHART.NET

CONTENTS

INTRODUCTION

PART 1:
BECOMING CASH-CONSCIOUS

PART 2:
FROM SALE TO CASH

PART 3:
"C" IS FOR "COERCION" –
COLLECTION & COURT

———————

PART 4:
WRONG IDEAS ABOUT RECEIVABLES

———————

PART 5:
IT'S ABOUT YOUR ATTITUDE

PART 6:
THE CUSTOMER IS ALWAYS…
THE CUSTOMER

PART 7:
AN OUNCE OF PREVENTION

PART 8:
TOOLS OF THE TRADE

PART 9:
THE CHASE IS ON!

POSTSCRIPT

INTRODUCTION

1. GETTING TO KNOW YOU

This is a book about commercial receivables – how to think about them, what to do with them and who should manage them. It's intended for owners, financial officers, controllers and senior managers of micro, small and medium size businesses that supply goods and services on credit terms in the Canadian and U.S. market. More specifically, it's directed at business people, established or just starting out, who are concerned about receivables performance and how to institute best practices in their cash-recovery strategies.

What it's not is a knee-deep-in-the-weeds "how-to"

manual meant for the desks of receivables clerks. WHERE'S MY CASH?! is designed to engineer or *re-engineer* your big-picture attitudes to this essential but often neglected area of business operations. You will be reminded that receivables matter, why they matter and how being cash-conscious today and every day is an integral feature of business health. And you'll be hearing it all from an expert theoretician and practitioner who's spent two decades in the A/R trenches of businesses just like yours.

The knowledge you will glean here emerges from real-life business experience in real-world companies. Practicality, convenience, empowerment and success will guide the exposition. It's my goal to convince you that effective, productive receivables are the *right and responsibility* of every enterprise, large or small. There's no magic bullet when it comes to getting paid, but there's no mystery, either. That's because not getting paid is not a viable option. Accounts receivable management is a mountain that every commercial business has to climb every day. It takes focused attention and concerted effort, just like any other aspect of business life, but receivables competence is attainable by every owner and executive who's motivated to make his or her company the very best it can be.

Helping you achieve this competence *is* what these pages are all about. And I'm dedicating them to you.

Cash is oil – so let the cash flow!

2. GETTING TO KNOW ME

I'd like to think it was inevitable. One day, I was *definitely* going to write this business book. And now that day has come. Destiny!

To tell you the truth, I can't remember a time in my life when I wasn't writing *something*. In fact, it was a broad range of "somethings," beginning with child-hood letters to my grandparents in Dublin and London, high school projects, then academic work at university and in full adulthood, magazine articles, TV episodes, screenplays and songwriting. Writing, it seems, comes as naturally to me as... breathing. As if I was put on this earth to put pen to paper and apply fingers to a keyboard.

It's been a parallel life – all this writing and working. And it continues without let-up today. So it's no surprise that, eventually, my urge to capture, classify, categorize and explain in print would seek the hand of my business expertise in marriage. A love-match made in my busy office over the course of eight long months of painfully early mornings and sandman-fighting nights.

Perhaps it's more accurate to say that receivables management was "the life apart." For many years, it was cash-recovery by day and writing by night. Weekends were a dead heat. I worked *and* I wrote. I look back on it now and wonder where I got the energy and discipline to live two lives 80 hours a week: money-chaser and struggling writer. I suppose it was pure love and a sense of duty. Or is that just the language of the backwards glance? Sometimes, it doesn't pay to dissect your own life. You just accept it for what it is and keep moving. Like a shark.

But here's a true confession: I came to receivables work by a combination of accident and serendipity. I had no special aptitude for numbers. I was never a good or engaged math student. And I didn't have an abiding love for business or the profit motive. In fact, I came from a generation that was congenitally suspicious of the "capitalist" ethos of the business world. The campus crews of the '60s were everything but commerce-positive. So how did I get here? How did I morph into an expert in the theory and practice of commercial receivables? To cite a Robbie Robertson song:

"The wind just kinda pushed me this way."

During the late '80s, I was working in Toronto for a national media association with a tightly-wound membership of business and trade magazines. It was an interesting environment, but that was just gravy. The job's main function was to support my nightly writing addiction and my wife's graduate studies. After a time, it became clear that the association's president was about to retire and his successor was scripting me out of the incoming regime. Things were looking grim.

Coincidentally, one of the member publishers with whom I'd built up a good rapport offered me the opportunity to switch horses just before mine got shot out from under me. All I had to do was to run her company's accounts receivable department. And with that one phone call, to which I said "yes" without much reflection, began a work-journey of 20 years. Magazine receivables, technology receivables, sub-trades receivables – all kinds of receivables! But all with one common commercial thread: goods and services supplied on credit; timely payment required.

I'm sure you've heard that great salespeople are born, not made. Is it true? Maybe so, maybe not. But I can tell you one thing for certain: No one was *born* to be an accounts receivable manager! No one came into this grumpy world of credit and cash for the expressed purpose of chasing unpaid commercial invoices. That's a learned skill. It's a toolbox that has to be built, tool by tool, during long years of discovery and more than just a few wrong turns into blind alleys.

Achieving expertise in cash-recovery is like achieving expertise in any other field of endeavour. It takes time, a lot of trial-and-error education and, if you're lucky, a few good teachers along the way. I was *very* lucky. I had great teachers when I was starting out. There were many insightful, generous CAs, controllers, CFOs and CEOs who taught me well. I'm grateful to each and every one of them. Thanks to their careful, patient pedagogy, I've never stopped learning about the ways and means of getting paid. I'm still waving the flag they gave me long ago.

Money, money, money! The relationship between people and money is one of the formative modalities of human civilization. Is it any wonder that the often murky process of payment is as varied and as variable as the people who have to be "encouraged" to pay what they owe? And that's what keeps it evergreen for me. That's what keeps me growing into my expertise. Hardly a week goes by when I don't have some unexpected "aha" moment about human nature vs. the almighty buck. And that goes for both sides of the payment equation. Understanding the expectations and the fears of creditor businesses that need to get paid is just as important and necessary as understanding the mindset of those who have to do the paying.

Business life is a big chessboard. Play on, my friends! But let's play smart. How smart? Well, let me put it this way: a good receivables manager is part-cop, part-lawyer, part-detective, part-psychotherapist. It's engaging work, that's for sure. Is it always *pleasant* work? No. That would be too much to ask for. But doing the job right tends to reduce the unpleasantness that prevails when you get it wrong. So now, two full decades after I started, whether I jokingly refer to myself as "Dr. Kash" or "The Sheriff of Cash County" or more seriously as "The Voice of the Money," it all boils down to this: I've become a veteran business "quarterback." I'm QB1 for the Cash flow Team. I quarterback commercial receivables on the gridiron of day-to-day business. And I like to win.

Have I seen it all? (Yawn.) No, but I've probably seen most of it, so I really do know why some businesses get paid while others don't. And while this book doesn't have a lot of kissing, it's got a whole lot of commercial telling. I'm sharing the distilled truths of commercial cash-recovery. Everything I know I've gleaned from experience – the experience of turning pastdue invoices into cash in the bank. If I can take that knowledge, invest it in these pages of "testimony' and help give your business the receivables performance it deserves and requires, then I've done my job. Touchdown!

And if there's a better business boast than that, I haven't encountered it yet.

3. ON THE PLATFORM

This is a "subway" story. It's about you and your business...

Every morning, you take the subway to work. Being a creature of habit, you come down the same escalator and wait at the same spot on the platform. When your train arrives, you select the same car and take the same seat. And you get out at the same stop.

Your escalator, your spot, your car, your seat, your stop. Day in and day out, it's always the same. "Nothing wrong with that," you say. "Routine makes perfect." No argument from me. But let's look at the analogy: your work life...

You have a pivotal role within your company. You've perfected it during years of paying close attention to detail. You have a routine way of doing things and a routine way of understanding the whole as a sum of parts. And it works. You know your job, and it shows. The downside? It can all become a little one-dimensional. You experience your company through the prism of your job-description, your title, your office. You see your business with one set of eyes and hear it with one pair of ears. Again and again. Day after day. It's natural, and it's also monochromatic. What's the risk? Leadership tunnel-vision.

WHERE'S MY CASH?! is *my* subway story. It places you on a different part of the subway platform. I want you to experience the subway from my perspective – from the point of view of a receivables manager and money-chaser. Sure, I take the same train you do, and I get off at the same stop, but the similarities end there. I wait at the far end of the platform, and I take a different escalator to get there. I have a different perspective on the happenings in the station because of my location. My vantage-point shows me different views. And when the train rolls in, I board a different car and take a different seat. Sometimes, if it's crowded, I prefer to stand.

My subway car is called "Cash." Yours is "Sales." As a receivables manager, I experience your company differently than you do, but it's the same company. So, come on down to my end of the platform and sit a spell, friend! Spend a few hours in these pages. Encounter your business from the point of view of your Accounts Receivable department. Witness your enterprise through a cash-recovery prism.

Welcome to my platform; welcome to my world. We know "The Question" already. Let's ask it together:

"Where's my cash?!"

Now, let's get busy with the answer...

BECOMING
CASH-CONSCIOUS

4. DEFINING ACCOUNTS RECEIVABLE

Defining terms is always a good place to begin. We have two options, two definitions.

In terms of business structure, Accounts Receivable (with capitals) is a department or module responsible for the status and outcome of company invoicing. Accounts Receivable has a cash-seeking mandate. As soon as an invoice is generated, it falls under the jurisdiction of the A/R unit. Whether it's one controller or one clerk in a small business or a platoon of money-chasers in a larger enterprise, this section of a commercial business is tasked with the responsibility of making sure that billings get paid.

That's the institutional definition. To your customers and your A/R staff, however, accounts receivable (without capitals) are simply unpaid invoices. These "receivable" amounts – *receivables* – are...

...monies owed to your company for goods or services already provided on credit.

By granting credit to your customers, you've agreed to supply your company's products or services in return for deferred but scheduled payment. You're waiting to receive payment. However, that payment is purely promissory. Yes, you'll *probably* get paid, but there's no absolute guarantee. Every invoice is subject to risk – the risk of receivables failure: non-payment. And despite the fact that your company requires predictability in its cash-recovery timetable, even when the promise of payment *is* fulfilled, there's no certainty about payment *timing*. It falls to your A/R manager to police both payment and timing.

When a business takes full payment at the point of sale, it produces no receivables. Pure retailers, for instance, offer no credit terms. They operate on a cash-on-the-counter or "cash-and-carry" business model. Retail goods or services are paid for immediately, and the cash-register receipt serves as a "paid" invoice. In contrast to retail payment, commercial receivables are characteristic of companies that refer to themselves as "suppliers" or "vendors." Nuances vary, but I'll be using these terms interchangeably. Typically, suppliers/ vendors extend credit to their customers because their competitors do. They *have to*; it's industry standard. But because only companies that bill *on credit terms* have accounts receivable, only businesses with receivables to recover require a unit to ensure receivable inflows.

5. REMEMBER THE FORGOTTEN ASSET

Whether practical or theoretical, there's no shortage of business books and website tools devoted to the main modules of commercial life: sales, marketing, accounting, customer service, leadership, human resources, image, branding, media training and – well, you name it! Every function gets its day in the sun, it seems, with one notable exception: receivables. Search the business shelves of your favourite bookstore or reconnoiter the online world and you'll be hard-pressed to find any substantive information about accounts receivable and cash-recovery management. Why is that?

Why is it so hard to access expert "intel" about such an imperative aspect of business life? After all, we're not taking about changing the kitty litter for the warehouse cat. That's a job nobody likes or wants. Fine. But we're talking about the place where the *money* lives! The money zone is always strategic. Monies we're owed are not a take-it-or-leave-it affair; they're mandatory. So, you'd expect there to be plenty of good guidance available on the topic. But there isn't. It's as if there's a grand, global conspiracy to forget the importance of getting paid because everyone worldwide agrees it's a subject that makes biz-life prickly and uncomfortable.

Question:
What are the four topics of conversation no business owner wants to have with customers?

Answer:
Sex. Politics. Religion. Unpaid invoices.

The phrase "forgotten asset" was coined many years ago to describe precisely this problem. According to the established principles of accounting, accounts receivable are an "asset." But they're an asset that gets neglected and marginalized. That's because senior management's focus is frequently directed elsewhere, typically to sales. Businesses compartmentalize receivables negatively, assigning them low-status and low priority, usually because they don't really know what to do about them. Remember the kid-sister none of the neighbourhood boys wanted in the Saturday schoolyard ballgame? Picked last, always with reluctance, and then stuck in outfield and ignored – Little Miss Invisible. When receivables are treated like they're *kid-sister-invisible*, we can infer that company leadership is either ill-informed or suffering from avoidance behaviour. Frequently the latter.

Too many business owners and senior executives are uneasy with their A/R responsibilities, and this lack of comfort promotes an almost willful forgetfulness. Yet, it's these very companies that suffer in the long run because cash is a vital business organ. Like a heart or a brain or a blood-supply. No supplier can survive long term without receivables competence. Becoming and remaining cash-conscious is a necessary quest. But how do we rise heroically to the occasion? The best antidote to forgotten asset syndrome is to consciously foster an A/R comfort zone. Careful education about receivables and how to manage them will make those crucial obligations to cash flow feel less alien and more familiar. And in any well-run business, familiarity breeds empowerment, not contempt.

6. THE MONEY MONARCH

You hear it all the time – that durable business cliché:

"Cash is king."

Of course, it got to be a cliché by being an unvarying truth. For those of us who toil in the for-profit universe, it's a proven commercial axiom. Cash is the lubricant that keeps all the working parts of a profit-seeking business in motion. It's the star on top of the commercial Christmas tree; it's the uncontested, universal measure of entrepreneurial success.

Your personal reward is bringing a great product or service to market and watching your clientele grow "royally" as your success gains traction. Making a difference on Planet Earth, no matter how your company makes that contribution, is an unalloyed pleasure. It's meaningful, and maybe it's what makes you tick as a human being. But the reward your business thrives on is big cash on the balance sheet. And the best method for getting that cash to where it needs to be is to systematically recover it from your receivables.

---

7. THE WAREHOUSE PROBLEM

Let's try it again...

"Where's my cash?!"

This may well be the most important question in your company's suggestion box. Where's the "green"? And if you have to ask, then we know where it's not: in your bank account.

Receivables that aren't fattening your purse are hiding somewhere else. But where? Where you've left them: in your customers' bank accounts.

"What percentage of our company's receivables can we afford to warehouse in our customers' bank accounts?"

Good question. Think about it. That's what unpaid invoices are: your cash warehoused with your clients. How does all this warehousing benefit your bottom line? It doesn't.

You already know that your business allies are closely watching your receivables. Your accounting firm, commercial lender, bonding agent and other business mentors – they all want the best for you. They're in your corner; they glory in your success. But they also monitor your company's financials to gauge that success accurately. And one of the key indicators of financial wellbeing is your receivables.

Your allies know that the fatter and older your receivables are, the less cash you have on-hand for meeting standard payables, paying insurance premiums, repaying and retiring loans, squaring tax obligations, R&D, payroll, and more. They also know that well-aged receivables get harder to recover as time passes. Risk escalates as the clock ticks. They'll evaluate your company's credibility, and by extension, your personal business acumen, using a variety of measures, not just cash, of course. But make no mistake, one of the most telling measures in their assessment will be cash-warehousing and its negative impact on your cash flow.

8. DOUBLE TROUBLE

When too much of our cash is warehoused with our customers, the double-trouble scenario is put in play: receivables high, cash low. Being ineffective on the A/R side leaves our businesses habitually cash-poor and constantly challenged by outflow requirements. Our payables are on the march in the wrong direction: upward. Creditors are phoning, faxing, emailing, and they're doing it daily. Everyone wants to be paid *first*. Everyone wants to be paid *now*. And what about the tax man, payroll and everything else?

This is immensely painful stuff to endure day in and day out. It's like a chronic illness we just can't shake. Not surprisingly, we find ourselves beleaguered, brooding and feeling panicky and inadequate. We mutter to anyone who'll listen:

"We have strong sales. Our customers owe us plenty of money. So why are we on our way to becoming a debtor business?!"

Exactly!

9. DOUBLE CRUNCHES

With receivables high and cash-recovery low, our companies begin to feel that crunch: cash-crunch. In search of day-to-day liquidity, we draw down on the company line of credit. But that's money that *costs* money. And what if the credit well starts to run dry? We go cap-in-hand to our lender's lair to request a credit increase. That's an appeal that can easily go wrong. There's every chance we'll hear that our receivables are too fat and too aged. Increase denied! And if that's not misery enough, we might even be warned of an impending *reduction* in access to credit if we don't pull up our cash-recovery socks. So, now, it's credit-crunch, too.

Wow, we're in a real bind now! We're peering over the edge! We contemplate "borrowing" from the tax account or selling-off equipment or a reduction in staff. And that's just for starters. Needless to say, none of these "solutions" are desirable, and some are truly drastic. They're also entirely unnecessary if our companies' cash needs can be positively addressed by managing our receivables more effectively.

See that rainbow on the horizon?

10. POT OF GOLD

I'm not suggesting that a commercial business should be able to live off its receivables *alone*. That would be one fortunate business – a genuine red-ribbon, open-field cash-cow. Nevertheless, owners and executives do need to recognize that cash-crunch and credit-crunch are avoidable if they know how to find their pot of receivables "gold."

Once a business becomes cash-conscious, the finance ball starts rolling in the right direction. Dams disappear; the cash begins to flow. Seeking positive results, new questions surface...

"Given our company's individual identity and operational characteristics, which policies will maximize cash-recovery?"

...and...

"Which procedures will give us the best shot at consistently productive cash-recovery from our monthly battery of invoices?"

These are definitely the right questions – and not the only ones. Here's another:

"If we commit ourselves to serving the money monarch, who's going to make that happen at ground-level?"

11. MOVING THE MONEY

If "who" refers to a job category, the answer isn't complicated. But when it means "which specific individual," then that's a human resources query.

As a job category, it's a straightforward proposition. Every supplier needs a competent receivables "mover." Someone has to push'n'pull the levers of the receivables "forklift." In general, the size of a business, its billing volume and the robustness of its credit management policies will dictate whether or not a full-time receivables manager is required. If that level of staff position is unnecessary or unworkable, then the part-time prospect is the one to explore. Perhaps there's an existing employee who can be seconded to receivables as a part-time A/R clerk. Or maybe a part-time A/R consultant brought in from the outside will prove the better fit. Regardless of who mans the A/R levers, it's the regime – the system – that counts. Competent, routinized receivables supervision trumps the warehouse problem by moving the money from the wrong warehouses to the right one. From our customers' bank accounts to our own.

WHERE'S **MY CASH**?!

FROM SALE
TO CASH

12. THE WHOLE-CAR PRINCIPLE

A thought experiment. The "whole-car" principle…

I want you to think of your business and its operational stream as a spiffy, street-legal vehicle. Your well-designed, well-maintained ride has a front end and a back end. Both ends are necessary because the car is a single entity. But if you neglect one end or the other, your ride is useless. You're not going anywhere. You've got to *service* the whole car because you've got to *drive* the whole car.

Your business has a front end and a back end, too. The front half is your products or services, sales and delivery. The back half may not seem quite as sexy because it doesn't have that muscular "motor" – sales – under the hood. But it's just as significant. Your sales team brings you customers. That's crucial to any business. And the back end? That's where you'll find your invoices and customer service/retention. But most of all, the back end is where your cash resides. It's your oil well.

Most entrepreneurs and their enterprises are front end loaded. They're sales-driven. It's a commercial necessity. But no business gets much drive-value out of having two fully-inflated tires up front and two flat ones in the rear. The whole car principle reminds us that to be truly "road worthy," a business must be integrated, with sales and cash receiving equal consideration and respect from company management.

13. TWIN ENGINES

To emphasize the point, I'm switching metaphors. Now, I want you to imagine your business as a train with twin engines. All aboard!

On your business train, both engines propel the enterprise forward. One pulls from the front; the other pushes from the rear. They only work optimally when they work together. In tandem, they gobble up those miles of commercial activity and speed your company down the track to your chosen destination: the golden kingdom of profit and growth.

The engine up-front is, of course, sales: making the sale; ensuring delivery. Whether your company supplies a product or provides a service, there has to be a sales engine hauling the freight or there's no business at all. Let's hear it for sales and your salespeople! And the engine in the rear? Receivables. It's the iron-horse of cash, and cash always has a cheering section. A perennial favourite and crowd-pleaser! Flow, cash, flow!

Sales and receivables are the two most important items of rolling stock in the Business Express. They make it possible for your product or service to get to market and fatten company coffers. Toot-Toot-Toot!

_____

14. BUILDING BLOCKS

_____

It's no state secret. There are four basic departmental components in the sale-to-cash process. They're not the only modules in your company's operations, but they're the ones that come to mind most readily when we think about the gears and pulleys of commercial enterprise. From an A/R manager's perspective, they're the company spine:

- Sales
- Shipping goods/delivering services
- Invoicing
- Receivables

15. RELAY RACE

It's a 4-stage relay, so don't drop the baton!

The sale-to-cash process is a linear route. It begins with a product order or service request which initiates a sequence of internal handoffs – from your sales office to your shipping or service staff, then to accounting, where an invoice is generated, and finally to your A/R manager, who ensures appropriate and timely payment. When your money-chaser crosses the finish line with glitter from the pot of gold, the sale-to-cash process comes to a successful close. A paid invoice seals it.

In any relay race, runner and baton have to cross the finish-line to win. The commercial contest also has a concluding rule. Until all four phases of the sale-to-cash process are accomplished, the sale is not complete. The finish-line tape isn't broken.

A satisfied customer and a satisfied receivable –
that's the commercial definition of victory.

16. MANAGING RISK

Because Murphy's Law applies to every business and every sale, there's always the possibility that something will go wrong in the commercial relay race. And it can happen in any part of the sale-to-cash sequence. Examples?

- A contract has "bugs," and those bugs change the payment outcome from getting paid to not getting paid the full amount or not getting paid at all.

- A quality-control failure results in the shipping of a defective product.

- A flawed service call makes an existing problem worse or precipitates a new one.

- An invoice turns out to be polluted by product/

service misinformation or incorrect pricing or tax codes.

- An inexperienced A/R clerk stumbles into a personality-clash with a client over late payment.

A single deal can also be afflicted with multiple glitches. Ouch!

Fubars like these will spoil any business day. They don't bear thinking about – except for the fact that we *have to* think about them. They're the risks we have to plan for daily. We have to expect the unexpected, as counter-intuitive as that may seem to the logical business mind. Blind-eye management profits no one; owners and executives who don't consider downside risk merely expose their businesses to *cash-tastrophe*.

It's only by being fully mindful of risk – what can go wrong and why – that we enable our companies to install best practices that minimize the chances of the wheels falling off one at a time or in unison. As a receivables manager, I'm always cognizant of the fact that getting paid in-full is dependent upon a range of factors embedded in the topography of a sale. A clean process, like a clean race, is likely to conclude fruitfully. So we go the distance. We dot the *I*s and cross the *T*s. We do everything possible and everything necessary to protect our receivables from risk.

Effective receivables are risk-aware receivables.

17. OLD-SCHOOL FOOTBALL

You've probably heard this oldtime football maxim more than once:

Put the ball in the air and three things can happen.
Two of them are bad.

Tried'n'true ball-sense. A pass can be caught. It can fall incomplete. Worse, it can be "picked" – intercepted by the other team. That's good, bad and worse. Only a 33.3% chance of a positive outcome. That's a lot of gridiron risk: 66.6%! And that's why risk-averse football coaches tend to favour the running game. What happens when you run the ball? Only two things – and only one of them is bad. Conclusion? The running game reduces risk.

This isn't "CFL On TSN," but I tossed out the football metaphor in the Introduction, so I'd better run with the ball now. I said I "quarterback" receivables. I do. That's my service work. But I'm also a consultant; I'm on the bench in a coaching capacity. This is a coach's book as much as anything else, so think of me as your offensive coordinator when it comes to cash-recovery play-making. I'm prowling the sidelines, looking for danger zones – places where you might get tripped, trapped or shoved out-of-bounds. I take a conservative, reduce-your-risk approach to A/R management. But I'm proactive. I *manage* commercial receivables risk. I don't just stand there with my hands in my pocket and watch risk happen. I build a winning receivables game plan to limit the things that can go south in the sale-to-cash process – things that cost my clients money and make them go grey before their time.

Like the risk-avoiding coach who wants to run the ball, my risk management playbook reminds you that every time you make a sale, two things can happen: either you'll get paid or you won't. There's no Mr. In-Between.

18. GETTING PAID…
NOT GETTING PAID

Got a preference? No-brainer there, right? You *want* to get paid. You *need* to get paid. Not only that, you want your clients to pay *voluntarily* – and on time, too. And many will do exactly that. Maybe even most. They're fair-play customers; they'll do the right thing. But too many customers have to be *told* to pay. They'll pay only on notice, often repeated notice, while others will make you play chase-the-weasel. And you'll chase some of them right into collection or small claims court.

Pastdue issues and ferret-chasing are all-in-the-game. Even with strong supervisory procedures and the daily application of best practices, the famous 80/20 rule applies in receivables as it does elsewhere. 80% of an A/R manager's time will be spent chasing 20% of the client base or 20% of the invoice inventory. And that 20% is a formidable pass-fail marker. Perhaps there are companies with cash reserves so deep that a 20% shortfall poses no fiscal jeopardy. But I bet there aren't many, and none of them have boards or shareholders to answer to!

19. LIFE WITH A/R MANAGEMENT... AND WITHOUT IT

Every commercial business gets to make this Hamlet-like choice:

To manage receivables efficiently and effectively – or not.

We can plant the flag of cash-recovery right on our doorstep. Or we can go without and hope that, come next Thanksgiving, our company won't be just another bankrupt turkey on a trustee's holiday plate. Isn't that just rolling the dice on company viability? You bet, but it's still a free choice – which might explain why there are always imprudent owners and executives hollering for sales, sales, sales while leaving their cash out in the cold.

Nobody's against full-blooded selling. I know I'm not. But I'd also like to see these business captains getting focused on cash, cash, cash. I'd like to see them get their receivables back indoors and huddled warmly around the company hotstove. That's where they belong. That's where they're needed most. And that's where they can do the most good.

20. BO PEEP'S FOLLY

Little Bo Peep, she lost her sheep,
And doesn't know where to find them.
Leave them alone, and they'll come home,
Wagging their tails behind them.
(or not)

Categorical statement heading your way... The Bo Peep method of A/R *non*-management doesn't work.

You remember Little Bo Beep, don't you? She's the nice kid in the next meadow who can't manage her flock of receivables. She's waiting, wishing, hoping for payment – and not doing much of anything else. Bo's management style – inactivity – is going to cost her dearly; she's not staying on top of her recovery problem. She's going to lose some "lambs." Predictable but also preventable.

Businesses replicate Bo Peep's folly when they wait

around for their dollars to come home like lost sheep. This is just glorified clock-watching. The days pass into weeks, the weeks into months, and the only thing that grows is the list of pastdue invoices and the bad debt allowance. Excuse me, but that's just hardway farm. Wring your hands and fret all you like, Bo Peep! It's passive agony in circumstances that cry out for brisk action.

If you're a sales-oriented owner, chasing receivables is probably the part of your business day you like the least. I understand why. It's the dirty end of the business stick. Maybe you'd like to avoid it altogether. I understand that, too. But I'm also telling you that, if you do, you've got it all wrong. You've got to be active in *every* facet of your business. You have to work at selling, and it's the same for cash-recovery. Commercial businesses have to wrangle their receivables. There's no way around it. No loafing in Bo Peep's waiting room!

Did I say that you have to *work at getting paid*?! I sure did, and I'm saying it again. Accounts receivable is an action-zone. Some portion of your invoices will always be subject to the money-chase. Maybe 15% this month. Maybe 20% next month. Is that the way business life *should* be? Perhaps not, but that's definitely the way it is. And in the real world of profit and loss, "is" trumps "ought" every day of the week. As long as there are customers that don't pay voluntarily, receivables require direct supervision. It's the *best* and *only* way to manage A/R risk.

---

21. CURVE AHEAD!

So how, exactly, do we manage risk in an A/R environment? By being thorough, methodical and consistent in a daily cash-conscious regime. Routine you can follow in the dark. A system that works just because it's systematic, and because systematic effort is the only effort worth a damn. And above all, by treating every single sale as if it has the potential for receivables failure. Which it does.

I realize that entrepreneurs are expected to be uniformly optimistic, but I beg to differ. Realistic risk management requires an outlook that's somewhat less rosy. When money's at stake, a little pessimism goes a very long way.

"Safeguard the peace by being prepared for war."

An archaic and controversial idea to some but a durable one with a long history of proofs. And it's as applicable to commercial activity as it is to conflict studies. When running a business, we're frequently called upon to be fortunetellers. We have to anticipate what's on the blind side of the curve ahead. And whether it's good or bad, we have to be ready to meet it. We plan ahead or get run over standing still.

22. SKUNK ALERT!

Becoming a vigilant shepherdess will help Bo Peep lure all those lambs from the back-40. And without getting skunked in the process. The analogy holds for your company and its receivables. Are there skunks lurking in your commercial meadow? *Mais oui!* When you provide goods or services on credit, you might *never* get paid. You might get *skunked*! Fact of life.

But risk management planning allows your business to reduce that skunking potential of bad debt. The logic is elegant. If you have to choose between getting paid and getting skunked, you don't have to think too hard about which is preferable. Once you decide "we're getting paid come hell or high water," you make a concerted ef fort to ensure that the building blocks line up to give you the right result. If products or services have been satisfactorily supplied at the agreed-to price, then the buyer who *won't* pay or *can't* pay has only two choices. He can go out of business, or he can tell-it-to-the-judge. In the first instance, your failed receivable is a write-off. Your customer is *kaputski*. In the second, you'll protect your receivable with coercion. If you can't finesse payment on an in-house basis, you'll push the chase to a new level – an external one. You'll assign the debtor to collection or take him to court.

23. THAT AWFUL SMELL

When that awful smell starts to permeate the air, it's because a supplier-client relationship has curled up in a corner and died. It's the smell of bad debt. Sometimes not even a collection assignment will shake the money tree; going to court may be the last best hope of rescuing doubtful cash.

Suit is the final stage of defense planning because legal remedy may be the only antidote to the odour of loss. No one relishes that eventuality. Court is no picnic, and it's far from a sure cure for debt. On the other hand…

A debtor whose business remains active and whose doors are still open can never be allowed to walk away from a legitimate, verifiable debt.

This is an article of faith I want every supplier to embrace. I want every vendor who comes up against a stubborn, uncooperative or uncommunicative non-payer to ask…

"If this deadbeat refuses to pay me, am I going to win my case in court?"

The rubber hits the road right here. This question is essential because thinking it through in its component parts obliges every business to adopt the policy standards and procedural safeguards that will ensure judgment in its favour.

Manage every sale as if it might end up in court.

Yes, it's commercial pessimism, but it's also effective. You may never need to appeal to the dotted *I*s and crossed *T*s of a contract, but on the day that pessimism-just-in-case turns out to be sadly justified, the *I*s and *T*s are your safety ducks-in-a-row. And there's a fortuitous upside. Those very same policies and procedures also happen to be *good business practice* generally, even if you're never forced to take a debtor to court.

Get organized! Get paid!

It pays to be organized and prepared on all fronts, and especially when money's on the table. Organized, well-managed receivables are successful receivables. And successful receivables are hallmarks of all profitable companies. Bad debt, on the other hand, takes dead aim at the bottom line. It's the sworn enemy of every profit-seeking enterprise. Make it your enemy, too. Stop the stink before it begins.

24. FOLLOW THE PAPERTRAIL

Can we backstop bad debt? All the time? Everytime? No, we can't. Not completely. But even though we can't unfailingly reduce it to zero, we can still make best efforts to minimize it. We can take positive action to mitigate the potential for receivables failure. In fact, that "can" is a "must."

In the previous chapter, I referred to "safeguards." By that I mean a system of preventative, prophylactic measures that form a barrier against receivables risk.

Follow the papertrail!

Whether documentation takes the form of electronic data or hardcopy in file folders, your company should produce a data trail for every product sale or service job. The trail may be long or short, substantive or thin, adequate or deficient, but there's going to be *some* flow of print information that explains the where, what, who, when, why and how of every sales event. This is the "papertrail." It's the written history of buy-and-sell. And it's your number one risk mitigator.

Following the papertrail is what you'll have to do to forge a well-crafted small claims case. A cogent, unambiguous papertrail persuades judges, and what persuades judges usually results in favourable legal judgments. With a strong papertrail to back you up, you've got the facts in your corner. You have a clear, orderly explanation of a debt you want remedied in court. You're in the right and can prove it, too. In the best of all possible worlds, you win your case.

The papertrail is your risk management *golem*. What kind of papertrail emerges form your business operations?

Let's take a look....

25. FROM YOUR SALES DEPARTMENT: Contracts, Deal Memos, Purchase Orders

We'll begin where all commerce starts: at the point-of-sale...

Every selling event has two dimensions: what was said and what's in print. In the final analysis, what-was-said is hearsay. Oral contracts may be legal, but try proving who whispered what to whom on mobiles or behind closed doors in the dark of a stormy night! Memories differ. Honest disagreements arise. And, unfortunately, some people will lie like stink if it suits them.

While a man's or woman's word may be his or her bond, a real-world checkdown proves that relying solely on verbal sales chatter is flawed procedure. He-said-she-said is an inexact, inefficient way to do business. It's not just false security, it's *no* security. No matter how persuasive it may seem in the glow of the selling moment, not even the most convivial sales schmooze can guarantee full payment at the end of the process.

Sales talk is cheap talk. It's what's in print – cool, definite print – that's going to define a sale legally and govern the recovery potential of any receivable.

A persuasive papertrail begins with your salespeople, or in the case of a service business, your order/dispatch desk. Whether it's a contract, quote, deal memo, work-order or a purchase-order provided by your customer, this is where the papertrail is born. These documents confirm what was agreed to at the point-of-sale. Vendor and client have acknowledged in *print* that they're on the same page about the arrangement – job-one in nailing down the legal conditions of the transaction and mitigating the potential for receivables risk.

26. FROM YOUR SHIPPING/SERVICE DEPARTMENT
Waybills & Service Sign-offs

Once the formative documentation leaves your sales office or dispatch desk, it floats downstream to your shipping or service department. Shippers will ship goods and service-providers will provide service on the basis of the *authority* of the papertrail created at the point-of-sale.

In due course, shipping and service confirmations become part of the accumulating record. They're instruments that add to the commercial narrative: the tale that the papertrail tells. They prove that goods were shipped or service was provided as per contract. They attest that your company has done what the sale documentation said it would do from the outset: fulfill its contractual obligations in return for a payment.

So where's that payment? Not so fast!

27. FROM YOUR ACCOUNTING DEPARTMENT
Invoicing

Since commercial payment is backended by credit terms, you have to hope that your customer will pay you and allow you to recover costs plus mark-up. You have to trust that the sales agreement will hold up. Meanwhile, inventory is waltzing out the door; service personnel are using parts and logging payable hours. One way and another, your company's expenses are on the rise, and they're rising solely on the *promise* of payment invested in the paperwork. If push comes to shove, this papertrail is your only guarantor of coverage.

Before you can get paid, you have to generate a payment stimulus. Something that tells your customer that the sale is coming to a close; something that reminds a client about the customer obligations invested in the contract. Now, before we go any further, let's give this hypothetical client a name. Let's call him "Customer Bill." We'll be seeing a lot of Bill in the sections that follow.

Once a product or service has been provided to Customer Bill in accordance with the contract, it's time to create an invoice. This invoice is your "request" that Bill fulfill his part of the sale agreement. You're informing him that (a) he's had the benefit of your goods or services and now (b) you expect to be paid by a specified date determined by the terms of credit.

All pertinent data required for billing Bill will be available to your order-entry clerk via the accumulated papertrail she receives from upstream in the company. She'll build it into the invoice, and that invoice, itself, becomes the central feature of the papertrail – the last and most perfect expression of the sale agreement. But remember that invoices age from the billing date. The credit clock begins its countdown as soon as the invoice comes off the printer, so send Bill the bill a.s.a.p. Don't delay. Timely billing matters. Is Customer Bill holding his breath waiting for your invoice to arrive? Is he salivating at his mailbox in keen anticipation of learning what he owes you? Is he desperate to write you that 4-figure cheque? Hmm... probably not.

The timing urgency in billing is yours, not Bill's. Bill's in no hurry. Why should he be? He's already got what he wanted: your product or your service. Being a competent and conscientious supplier, you satisfied Bill's need effectively and quickly. Now it's Bill's turn to do the satisfying. You need Bill's cheque, credit card authorization, money order or cash; Bill needs a giddy-up to kickstart the payment process. That's what the invoice does: it notifies. So, the sooner Customer Bill's invoice is on its way, the sooner Bill will know how much he owes and when payment is due.

Too often, it seems, invoicing is delayed. On Hectic Boulevard, every business is busy-busy. Every business is full of firefighters putting out fires 24/7. I know that and you know that. In pressed and pressured enterprises, the billing process can get sidelined for days, even weeks. And that's regrettable because delayed invoicing works against a supplier's cash requirements. King Cash is never served if invoices are trapped in a desktop and unable to get out of the printer. If your company's invoicing habitually takes 3, 4, 5 weeks just to reach a mailbox, that's a red flag snapping in a stiff, unforgiving breeze. What it's flagging are "timing-belt" issues within your sale-to-cash process.

When your billings are tardy, Customer Bill smiles. No invoice, no payment.

---

28. FROM YOUR
ACCOUNTS RECEIVABLE DEPARTMENT
Cash Reports, Proofs of Payment, Pastdue Notices

We've traced the papertrail through sales, shipping/service and invoicing. Next stop: Accounts Receivable. That's the department where we ask the age-old question:

"Uh...um...so when do we get paid?"

Every invoice has an individual timer: the credit terms established at the point-of-sale. Eventually that timer is going to sound-off. Credit time will expire; payment will be due when it does. *Receiving* that payment, of course, is another matter entirely. The papertrail for any sale concludes successfully only when payment is recorded in a cash report or some equivalent accounting document. And for any supplier who's ever faced an NSF payment, the sale really closes only when the cheque *clears the bank!* When there's no cash at the end of the line, there's no cash to close the invoice. The sale is unfinished and deficient. We're looking at a possible write-off. Fail!

Efficient A/R oversight, comprising review of invoicing, recording of payments and good "housekeeping" strategies, keeps your company's aging report clean and comprehensible. Sill, payment aggravation is a regular visitor to the receivables offices of even the best-run businesses. And it's at this point that an A/R manager enters the often edgy, psychological realm of pastdue pursuit. Good-cop. Bad-cop. Hand-holder. Therapist. Caped Avenger. Prison guard. The many masks of the money-chaser.

Receivables recovery presents a panorama of payment what-ifs. What if...
- ...you don't get paid on time?
- ...a problem client pays *habitually* slow?
- ...there's a delinquent that won't pay at all?
- ...you get paid short?

- …a bank debit fails?
- …you get stuck with a bum cheque?
- …a cheque is stopped or bounces?

Voluntary payment in sync with our credit terms is what we all want from our customers, but wishing doesn't make it so. If we don't get that good payment behaviour voluntarily, there are other alternatives. And we make good use of them. Delinquents with unpaid or shortpaid invoices *must* be contacted. Don't delay. No time to watch the glaciers melt.

Pastdue pursuit – the chase – *does* work. Over time and with application of systematic pastdue procedures, the majority of slow-payers will fall into line. Many will even stay in line. But there are always going to be non-cooperators. These difficult or lame duck clients need to know that you're totally resolved when it comes to getting paid. If they don't pay on the basis of the terms of credit, and they still won't pay after receiving pastdue reminders and phone calls, you'll just "graduate" their files. You'll let coercion rule. What you *won't* do is walk away. You don't quit on monies owed.

29. AT THE END OF THE TAIL
Collection Assignments, Legal Briefs

We've arrived at the tail-end of the sale-to-cash process. Communications from Accounts Receivable have been added to the papertrail. Copies of pastdue notices, emails, notes on phone calls and debtor responses – all of it will help your A/R manager craft a convincing legal case should you have to take a debtor to court. For many good reasons, however, court may not be your preferred option. At least, not at first. If you're a typical creditor, collection will be your first port-of-call. So when you assign a delinquent account to your preferred collection agency, your distilled papertrail becomes available to the collector working the file, and in turn, that collector's notes form a final add-on should the file "graduate" a second time – to small claims court.

WHERE'S **MY CASH**?!

"C" IS FOR "COERCION" – COLLECTION & COURT

30. TO THE WOODSHED!

If the word "collection" makes you shudder, that's appropriate. It should. Sending any customer "to the woodshed" goes against the grain, but sometimes, it's the only alternative. Who do we assign to collection? None of our good customers – no way! That's because there's no need to. Good customers are good payers; they're cooperative, timely and reliable. It's these customers we're thinking of when we proclaim:

"Our clients are our most valuable asset!"

We love good customers! We work hard to land them, and we work hard to retain them. We cherish their business. We don't play fast'n'loose with their loyalties, and we don't fire them without sufficient cause. We invite them to the company Christmas party, instead.

But what about that *other* kind of customer? The kind no one wants or needs. The kind we wouldn't wish on the dog catcher. Oh, those obstinate, troublesome, difficult, deceitful, slow-paying, non-paying, time-sucking, generically bad-to-the-bone customers! These are the only ones that belong on the firing line. We ship them to the woodshed with a "good riddance" on our lips; we suffer no pangs of conscience.

When we assign an account to a collection agency, what we're doing is "firing the client." It's a relationship-ender. The chances of that business liaison surviving the collection process are slim to zilch. And while no one wants to give customers the ol' heave-ho, collection agencies do have their place. They're valuable strategic allies with *uber*-chase talents most vendors don't possess. They can pull the financial fat out of the fire; they can make good things happen at the 11th hour. They're our game-saving bullpen. Nevertheless, collection is a last resort. We have to go along way down the road of in-house pursuit before we pull the plug and call in the collectors, changing the channel forever.

There are *customers* and then there are *debtors*. Even if Customer Bill isn't a beloved client in-good-standing, until you actually give up on him once and for all, he's still a customer, albeit one who owes money he's not paying. But let's say things don't improve. Let's say they go from bad to worse. Your receivables manager reports that Bill is dancing her around. She's lost faith in his willingness and ability to pay. She doesn't believe a word he says anymore. She's convinced Bill's a junk-client.

With wrinkled brow and consternation in your eyes, you face the unhappy facts. The cash-recovery efforts your people have poured into Bill's pastdue account have pancaked. Any additional time and energy your staff devotes to Bill's gamesmanship will be wasted. And what about opportunity cost? Your receivables people have more important and productive things to do. They have to move on and recover cash from compliant clients – clients who *will* pay.

After mulling it over, you conclude, correctly, that there's no more patience left to squander on Customer Bill. Every additional chase email or phone call costs you money. That's more money – your money – added to the invoice dollars he's not paying already! So, you ask yourself:

"Do I need this deadbeat on my customer list?
Do I really want to keep carrying an account that produces
nothing but aggravation and unpaid invoices?"

You don't. So good, it's decided! Customer Bill is now officially a debtor. Congratulations!

Firing a bad customer is a declaration of supplier freedom.

When a bad customer graduates to being a debtor, it's time for the woodshed. You authorize your A/R manager to assign Debtor Bill's account to a reputable, proven collection agency. What happens next? Your receivables manager will distill the papertrail she draws from Bill's pastdue file. She'll cherry-pick the important features of the documentation and write a concise report that will tell a collection agency everything they'll need to know about assignment. Well-informed, and armed with the right documents, they'll be able to take decisive, and hopefully successful, action on your behalf.

On one hand, providing an A/R commentary is just a simple courtesy to your agency-of-record; but it's also a matter of self-interest and self-defense. We ask collection agencies to help us defend our receivables by means that we don't have at our disposal, using time we're no longer prepared to invest. It's much to our advantage, therefore, to provide a collector with a clear explanation of debt. But that's the *last* thing we do.

Once your receivables manager has emailed or faxed the assignment, it's time to step back and let your agency do the work it does best. Remember, as far as you're concerned, the vendor-customer relationship is dead. Customer Bill shredded it when he forced to you fire him. You've handed-off the receivable to an external fixer. What you want now is cash-recovery by hook or crook. It's Bill's lookout, not yours, if he doesn't like what happens next. And chances are he won't.

Collectors aren't concerned with dead relationships. They don't have to be. They'll assume that any account you send their way is no friend of yours – not any longer. As the assigning client, you're entitled to relay your thoughts about "diplomacy" in your assignment memo. You can do the same in realtime discussions with the collection agency's sales rep. You outline your expectations and offer your impressions about the woodshed candidate. A responsive agency will welcome that input and do its best to take your cues into consideration.

What you *can't* do, however, is carry on separate negotiations with the debtor *after* the assignment has been filed. Collection agencies don't appreciate "triangular" assignments, and they have every reason not to. Many serial debtors are tricksters and evaders by nature. Collectors need to deal with them bilaterally, and they need to do it forthrightly, sometimes bluntly and without "other voices" piping up from the wings. Meaning yours. They expect good collection etiquette from assigning vendors.

Should a debtor try to do an end-run around the agency and re-open negotiations with the supplier, that vendor has to support the collection process by shutting the door.

"Sorry, Bill, that train has left the station. We've assigned your account to collection. It's out of our hands."

How can you be sure you've reached the end of the line in negotiating with a non-paying customer? When is it time to contact a collection house? Here are some useful clues:

The debtor…

- …is rumoured to owe money all-over-town.

- …reneges on a negotiated payment commitment and offers no remedy when pressed.

- …flunks a credit check with a credit reporting agency or other suppliers.

- …informs you that his business is circling the drain.

- …tells you he will *never* pay, no matter what you say or do.

- …stops communicating and won't to respond to your calls/faxes/emails/expedited mail.

- …"invites" you to sue him or recommends you take a long hike to Uranus.

- …threatens to take out a mob contract on you or your family (or some other equally nasty and actionable form of uttering).

Sound familiar? If so, go ahead – send 'em to the wood-shed! But there's a caveat. No matter how capable and persistent they are, collection houses can't work miracles. You've handed your agency a vexed file. That's what every collection assignment is: stressed and distressed. If it wasn't troublesome, you'd have brought home the bacon yourself. Your agency's collectors will work that file diligently. They'll make every effort to "influence" the debtor's thinking about the debt. With luck, they'll bring your ex-customer to heel, successfully shaking the money tree. But they may also come up empty-handed. And if a debtor proves impervious to woodshedding, your agency may recommend that you move to the next stage of coercion: a small claims action.

31. WHEN IT'S TIME TO SUE

Here's something worth meditating on:

At small claims court, winning isn't just the best thing, it's the only thing.

And another *bon-mot*:

In a small claims process, the only suit worth winning is one that will actually deliver cash.

Unfortunately, receivables recovery doesn't always turn out the way we'd like. Sometimes the weasel has gone to ground. Can't be found. Sometimes he or she wants to play "chase-me." No communication. And often a debtor flatly refuses to pay or consider a settlement. Not even a collector can shake out some coin. What to do now?

When things get to this point, a creditor is faced with two possibilities:

- abandon pursuit and write off the debt
  or
- go legal

By "going legal," I'm referring only to files that meet the small claims court (SCC) guidelines in your province. Maximum suit amounts, as well as other SCC criteria and procedures, vary from jurisdiction to jurisdiction. Debts that exceed SCC maximums are sued in a higher court and require legal counsel. Most readers of this book will be exposed to debts within SCC range. There's also a second consideration: invoice age. Your business may be registered in a province where invoices over 2-years old are grandfathered *out* of the legal frame. They're too *old* for court. As dead Marley's Ghost on Christmas Eve! Any collection agency worth its stripes will give you solid information on all these details. Alternatively, you can consult the SCC rules and regulations at the website of the Ministry of the Attorney-General of your province (or the province in which a case would have to be heard). Knowledge is power, so don't hesitate to arm yourself with as much of it as possible.

Let's assume that you've done your homework. You're satisfied that your unpaid invoice passes muster for a small claims chase. Right now, this is what's on your mind:

"Should I sue the delinquent or let it slide?"

If you have a burning desire to prove that you're "right" and the debtor is "wrong," a small claims court may *not* the place for you. It's totally understandable that you'd want to "educate" or punish a debtor who's made such an unmitigated nuisance of himself, as well as depriving you of your own cash. You may also want to send a message to others in your industry about your intention to uphold the integrity of your invoices. I'd like to be able to tell you that SCC is about justice triumphant and the right maintained, but as the Gershwin song says: "It ain't necessarily so!" Being in the right won't inevitably tip the scales of justice in your favour. Court is not a meritocracy. You don't win because you deserve to win. Going to court can be a laborious, time-intensive and intimidating process. And it's certainly not free. So scrutinize your motives for launching litigation *before* you take it on. Hindsight is the land of snowy regrets.

There are three factors that inform a decision to sue:

- win-ability
- debt-value
- access to post-judgment cash (or equivalent, e.g. property)

First: win-ability. You need a court case you can win. What's required? A clear-cut commercial narrative without "bugs." Persuasive documentation and the ability to present well at a settlement conference or trial. If there's anything iffy – e.g. contradictory documentation, a dispute over product or service or competing accounts of a verbal agreement – you'll have to reassess. Court is no place for sissies. It's also no place for winging it with a case that's not bulletproof.

Is the law debtor-friendly? I often wonder about this, myself. It's not supposed to be. Not in theory. Yet, in practice… Yes, SCC is the established legal venue that allows suppliers to sue for unpaid receivables. But it sometimes appears to be deliberately structured to give debtors every avenue of escape while making it as hard as possible for creditors to achieve redress. If your case is a leaky ship, you can forget about a positive outcome. You'll be a bird flying on one wing. At a settlement conference, for example, you may find that a weak position forces you to offer an unfavourable concession. Alternatively, you may achieve only a sawoff judgment at trial. In fact, you may lose outright and face court costs. That's adding insult to injury – and you'll have sent more good money chasing after bad! Who needs that!

But let's assume you have a strong case with a convincing papertrail. Additionally, you're feeling bullish about your presentation skills, written and oral. Good enough. But before you plunge ahead, please pay special attention to debt-value. Even if you have a solid, presentable case, you still have to assess whether the project meets the cost-benefit test:

Is suing Debtor Bill a sufficiently cash-positive proposition?

Does the maximum amount of money your company can reasonably expect to extract from the small claims process legitimize the time, the effort and the cash you're going to have to invest to secure the judgment? From the get-go, you'll need an exposure worth the hunt.

Suppose it costs you a total of $500 in legal fees to win either...

- a $500 settlement of a $750 receivable
  or
- a clear judgment on a $500 receivable.

Suppose further that the defendant, Debtor Bill, makes good on the $500 without a fuss. Would you think you'd actually "won" anything? Neither scenario is cash-positive. Both fail to justify the process; they're no-money propositions. Verdict: no-thanks.

Every time the possibility of suit arises, we have to ask whether the value of the claim validates the cost. Frankly, this is fatal news for small debts. No way to sugar-coat it, chasing small dollars through the courts is not a viable option. It's just bad news all around. The flowcharts for a tepid case or a minor exposure both end in a write-off.

It goes without saying that having to ditch a receivable is unappealing. It's morally offensive. It hurts our pocketbook and wounds our commercial pride. Nevertheless, there are times when a write-off is simply the *smarter* move. Here's a debt-value checklist to guide you in making your decision:

✓ How large is the debt?

✓ How much will it cost to chase via the courts?

✓ How much time and aggravation will have to be invested?

✓ What are the minimum and maximum cash benefit amounts that can reasonably be expected to emerge from the process?

Let's suppose you've got the waterfront covered. There's an exposure worth taking to court, and you've got a winning narrative. Unfortunately, even having a potent case with a significant debt-value isn't enough. You also need to consider what happens – or *doesn't* happen –

after you win a judgment.

- Does the debtor have any assets with which to satisfy judgment?

- Are those assets accessible?

- If the debtor refuses to satisfy the judgment, how much time, money and effort will be required to "action" that judgment?

What's the object of the exercise? You're going to court for financial remedy. You want to get *paid*. That's the litmus test: *getting paid*. You're not going down this arduous road just to prove a point or gain a pyrrhic victory. And if you can't get paid no matter what you do or how justified you might be, what's the practical value in making it a court matter? Once again, King Cash must be served. Debtor Bill has led you and your collection agency on a merry chase. That's bad enough. But is he also the kind of unredeemable rascal who'd even squib away on a court judgment? If so, that will force you into a new and unwanted layer of legal pursuit: "actioning" the judgment. You'll be looking at additional costs in time, money and stress. And that's not all. Whether Debtor Bill is compliant or resistant may not even matter. Bill may not possess any accessible assets; he may be flat broke.

If there's no reasonable expectation of a payout,
there's no relief in court remedy.

But let's think positively. Let's imagine you've accurately assessed the situation regarding Debtor Bill's account. You've asked yourself all the right questions, come up with the right answers and given yourself a green light to proceed. The exposure warrants it, the case is open'n'shut and apparently Bill's company is not in the poor house. You're going to take the plunge. You're going to sue Debtor Bill in small claims court. Now what?

Having ruled out the services of a solicitor due to prohibitive costs, you have three options to choose from:

- collection agency
- paralegal services
- self-management

At least one of them will be right for you. But which one? Let's investigate…

Your Collection Agency Ally

When it comes to most small claims cases, I'm biased in favour of collection agencies. As far as I'm concerned, it's almost always the happiest fit. However, much like A/R managers, collectors also hit the wall from time to time. Despite all the agency's best efforts, an assigned debtor proves unresponsive, non-compliant or pleads poor in perpetuity. When that happens, the agency will contact you and offer advice about the next step. What will you hear?

You may be told that the agency prefers to close the file and advises you to do likewise. That's usually because they feel that…

- …the invoice value is too low to justify further expense.

- …the papertrail isn't strong enough to support a winning court case.

- …the debtor is untraceable, insolvent or legally bankrupt.

- …the debtor company is a hollow shell – an asset-less corporation that's effectively out-of-business.

Closing the file means a write-off and bad debt. Game over. Where there's a bankruptcy, you may still be able to file a proof-of-claim with the managing trustee. But that's generally a cold-comfort proposition. Since your business is very likely to be an unsecured creditor, the chances of seeing anything but a few cents on the dollar at best are remote.

On the other hand, your agency may consider a small claims suit a practical venture, in which case you'll receive a permission-to-sue letter. This letter is a recommendation that you empower the agency to move the assignment from their collection department to their legal team. That team which will initiate a claim on your behalf. If you authorize your agency to proceed, their suit-squad will navigate the file through the small claims process to whatever its conclusion may be: win, lose or draw. You'll be updated regularly, and you can abandon the case at any point without penalty.

What are the advantages of going legal via your collection house?

Your agency...
- ...is already acquainted with the file from the collection phase
- ...offers a legal department with expert staff
- ...has years of experience in managing SCC cases

A proficient collection agency gives any creditor an excellent opportunity to platform a winning court case. This doesn't assure success every time out, however. What happens in a small claims courtroom can be unnerving; it can even inspire disbelief. But generally speaking, if you give your agency a burly file and a debtor with reachable assets, the chances of a positive outcome are pretty reasonable.

Take note of the downside, however. Of the three options, the agency route is often the most expensive. I'm paying a premium for a professional service. Is this a significant negative? Not really. As a creditor, I want it done right. I want to see cash at the end of the legal tunnel, and I'm willing to pay for know-how and convenience to make it happen. If greater expense ensures me a smart, well-managed suit that isn't going to suck my time and energy and tax my legal knowledge, and if it's also my best shot at seeing some return on a troubled receivable, then that's the way I'm going to go. I'm going to walk hand-in-hand with the experts and keep my eyes on the prize.

Regardless of whether you receive encouragement to sue or a recommendation to abandon, you're not required to do either. You're not obligated to use the agency's legal services, nor are you compelled to walk away from the debt. You can still proceed with suit on a self-managed basis or via a paralegal. But an agency's negative opinion on a difficult or doubtful file is probably authoritative. A loser is a loser is a loser. When the dead begin to smell, we bury the bodies.

If a collection house advises you to let them take the debtor to court, be aware that you'll have to provide front-money. Collection is a contingency environment; agencies take a back end percentage of monies received from debtors. But once it's a legal file, front end funding becomes necessary; collection agencies do not finance their clients' legal forays. Be sure to ask your agency sales rep. about the costs of filing suit and the contingency percentage applied to legal files, and do it in advance of making your decision. The permission-to-sue letter will likely make everything explicit, but no creditor should feel shy about asking for precise details.

Typically, the initial fee is a draw-down amount used

for staged disbursements as the agency manages the initial phases of the suit. As a rule, this fee will cover normal expenses through pre-trial to an uncontested or "default" judgment. A creditor will incur additional costs, however, if the debtor defends the suit and the case goes to mediation or trial. Extra expense will also come into play if it becomes necessary for a paralegal or a company representative to appear at a conference or trial on the plaintiff's (aka complainant's) behalf. And should a debtor refuse to satisfy a court judgment, and the creditor opts to "action" that judgment, costs will most certainly escalate.

"Actioning" a judgment is no walk in the park. Winning a judgment isn't winning tax-free cash; it's not the 6/49. A judgment is only a ticket-to-ride; it's a legal lever that guarantees nothing beyond your right to make use of it as best you can. A debtor may satisfy a judgment without undue resistance and rancor. That definitely makes life easier. But often enough, it's just more of the same – more avoidance, more resistance, more chase. Actioning is the chase-after-trial, and it can be annoying, dispiriting and costly. Worse yet, there's no certainty of tapping into a vein of silver.

I don't want to get much deeper into the weeds of small claims suits because details vary, depending upon specific agency protocols and provincial SCC norms. All the same, we should review some of the price-points of an agency-managed suit.

For instance, that $500 in legal fees I mentioned earlier. It's nothing to sneeze at. $500 is probably on the high side, although it's not incredible by any means. Costs will vary by region and province, and some agencies will be more cost-competitive than others. Overall, however, there's probably a reasonably narrow range of difference. My favourite collection agency in Toronto, for instance, has a $400 opening fee. Let's go with that figure. $400 buys a seat at the table.

You can certainly ask a judge or magistrate to fold court costs and pre-trial interest into a judgment awarded in your favour, but the drop-charge will never be directly recoverable. You can't add it to the suit amount; it's just out-of-pocket money priming the legal pump. Legal fees are best treated as a cost of doing business: a legitimate business expense. The same holds true for collection agency commissions. Now, about those commissions…

As I said, collection agencies operate in a contingency environment. They take a commission on all monies recovered on our behalf, whether via collection or the litigation they manage for us. If they don't succeed, they don't get paid. That's the essence of the contingency model. I can't speak for all agencies, but my preferred agency operates with a 25% commission on collection accounts of the type most small or medium sized businesses would throw their way, provided the invoicing is less than one year-old. And the percentage rises to 33% if the file goes legal. Other agencies may operate with rates that are somewhat higher or lower. Again, research required on your end; you may find interesting variations.

Commission obligations degrade the dollar-value of the receivables we assign. Using 25% as a standardized rate, the moment we convey an assignment to a collection agency, our receivable, if collected in-full, will decline to 75% of its book-value. That's not how our internal accounting will render it, but that's the ground-level reality. The cash-recovery ceiling of the assigned invoice is lowered by one-quarter. In the best-case scenario, we'll recover 75% of the value of the invoice and expense the remaining 25% to a GL (general ledger) account for collection agency commissions.

Adopting a 25% contingency rate for collection success and 33% for an agency-managed win in court, here's a little guerrilla math:

If we assign a $1000 receivable, and our agency secures the full amount via collection activity, we'll see $750 and post a $250 commission expense. But if that same $1000 receivable goes legal, and we're fortunate enough to (a) gain a full judgment and (b) have a debtor that pays without further chase, we'll receive $670 and book a commission expense of $330. But since there may be extra dollars tacked on for trial costs and pre-trial interest, the $1000 judgment escalates to, say, $1200. In that event, we'll receive about $800, expensing approxmately $400 to a commission account.

But what if it's already cost us up to $500 to get that $800 return? A $300 benefit? Is that really what we went through all the hassle for? While we'll be able to expense the $500 in legal fees plus the $400 commission, we'll still be netting less than 1/3rd of the book value of the receivable. One-third recovery isn't totally shabby – not compared to 0%, which is what would happen if you just wrote-off the invoice without further pursuit. But as a best-outcome proposition, it begs reflection. Is it really worth it? Probably better than writing off a $1000 account without a fight – but that's about the best that can be said.

I reiterate: small debts make poor legal targets, and they're not cost-effective in an agency environment. Collection agencies understand this, so you'll discover that most of the larger houses have a minimum debt-value for legal process. Below that minimum, a file is not of interest as a court prospect. No worthwhile gain for creditor or agency. A lot of effort for very little cash.

Your Paralegal Ally

Can we reduce the costs of suit and enhance recovery value? Could paralegal services be a better option?

A paralegal (or court agent) is not a solicitor, but he or she will have court experience, legal knowledge and a professional designation confirming that he/she has received formal training in the field. An expert para-legal can be relied upon to serve as your standard-bearer in a small claims procedure. You'll be well-advised and well-supported. Of course, you'll have to provide a paralegal with organized and coherent documentation. That's no different than it would be with an agency assignment. And if your paralegal agrees that you have a worthwhile, workable case, he/she will see you through to the end of the process, be it bitter or sweet.

Unlike collection agencies, paralegals don't charge commission, they're legal consultants who work on a fee-for-service basis. You'll still have to cover all the usual disbursements: filing fee, process service charges, trial fee and any and all other legal expenses that come down the pike. And if travel is required, travel costs and per diems will come into play, as well. So when shopping for paralegal services, always request a complete inventory of fees and costs before signing on.

Let's suppose that you've paid your paralegal's opening fee, and he/she has filed your claim and is monitoring its progress. If the debtor files a defense, the case will likely have a settlement phase. A settlement conference is a court-mediated meeting to determine if compromise is possible before going to trial. (The court's objective here is to avoid a trial, if at all possible.) In this situation, a paralegal may require a secondary fee for his/her attendance. If a settlement is not reached and the case goes forward, another service increment will be needed, along with the trial disbursement. And should your paralegal have to action a judgment on your behalf, further service fees will be charged in addition to process expenses such as seizure of debtor goods, funds or property by the sheriff's office. It's a stage-fare system, and it can add up over the life of a suit. But because paralegals don't take a back end percentage of cash-recovery, the paralegal route can still be a less expensive option than the agency-managed suit.

On the assumption that the legal disbursements you'll provide to a paralegal or to a collection agency are similar, if not identical, the salient question becomes...

How do paralegal service fees stack-up against agency commission?

The answer depends on the variables of a specific suit. If the case is complicated and drawn-out, paralegal fees will increase. More work means greater cost. But if the dollar value of a suit is substantial, the agency's commission will be significant. Bottom line? A complex, low-value suit isn't a good fit with paralegal services; a straightforward, high-value suit is.

Self-Managed Suit

There's still a third option to consider: managing a suit in-house. Yes, you and your staff can do all the legwork, all the filing and all the boning-up on the legal and procedural aspects of creating a coherent, win-able small claims case. In fact, this is how SCC is *supposed* to work. The People's Court. Citizen justice. Except that, increasingly, it doesn't and it isn't. For instance, it's extremely disconcerting to go to a settlement conference or trial and find a debtor "defended" by a gung-ho solicitor who runs rings around your claim and seems way too chummy with the presiding judge or magistrate. Currently, as SCC maximums rise in some jurisdictions to $25,000 and beyond, formal representation tends to become more frequent, if not the norm. Let's face it: the incentive is persuasive. There's a lot of cash on the line and only one good shot at getting it right. Whether creditor or debtor, it only seems prudent to reach out for expert help in the person of a lawyer or paralegal if the value of the claim is lush.

The main advantages of being your own case manager are reduced costs and, if you're really committed to the process and versed in small claims procedures, a sense of empowerment and accomplishment when you win. Some people are lawyer-wannabes. They represent themselves effectively and they don't mind the investment of time and effort. In fact, they *relish* it; they *enjoy* the process. But are you this kind of person? If you're not, is there someone in your company who is? If so, a self-managed small claims case may be just what the doctor ordered – and we'll politely ignore Mark Twain's tart observation that anyone who represents himself in court has "a fool for a client."

Questions to ponder before you go it alone?

- Are you and your staff the most effective agents of your company's interests when it

comes to taking a debtor to court?
Do you have sufficient expertise – preparation skills, procedural knowledge and in-court presentation moxie – to put it all together successfully?

- If you don't, are you willing to do what it takes to develop on-the-fly court proficiency?

- Estimate the time and uptake costs in a self-managed suit. Time is money, too.
  Do you have the time and the focus for the task?

If your responses are all enthusiastically affirmative, then by all means, go the distance; run your own suit. You'll save money in the end. You'll have court and related costs to cover, stage by stage, but you won't have to shell out for professional service fees or contingency commissions. And you'll get 100% of whatever you win. But let me inject a note of caution:

100% of nothing is still nothing.

To achieve the potential cost savings in a self-managed suit, you have to *win* your case. So if legal DIY is up your alley, go for it. But if the do-it-yourself approach is going to harm your chances for a successful suit, better bark up a tree with a specialist in it.

WRONG
IDEAS ABOUT
RECEIVABLES

---

32. RELUCTANT LEADERSHIP

Poor performance in accounts receivable will put any business in a bind. Sometimes company leadership is aware of the problem; sometimes they're not. And when they're not, they seem hamstrung. They're unable to pinpoint the cash flow difficulty. Unable to cut to the heart of the pain. Usually, it's a question of not knowing how receivables work and why they matter. But the solution is simple. Motivated leadership can avail itself of A/R education and then act on that learning. That's one way out of the truss.

Owners and executives who understand the problem they're facing but seem reluctant to take decisive action are a very different kettle of fish. In my early years as a money-chaser, I found it absolutely mystifying that a company's leadership would simply tolerate A/R pain, month after month, quarter after quarter, enduring substantial write-downs, year after year. The cure seemed obvious to me:

Work your *&@%^* receivables, for God's sake!

Why wasn't it obvious to them? What was I missing about what they were missing?

Over time, I began to listen more closely – and more

sympathetically – to companies that *didn't* "get it." Gradually, I started to identify roadblocks, speed-bumps and fallen trees on the highway to payment. Faulty thinking, wrong ideas, misplaced fear – they're all stumbling blocks to achieving effective receivables. And here they are. Totally naked! Some may resonate; others will make you angry if they hit too close to home.

33. SOCIAL RISK, SOCIAL RETICENCE

Just blame it on the social codex!

The "social codex" – the web of familial and social relationships – can be an intensely complicating factor. It's most likely to hold sway in small towns and small cities, but it's also found in metropolitan centres where businesses draw their clients from a close-knit socio-ethnic group or a delimited geographical area. When a social codex superimposes itself on a business environment, it's definitely a good-news-bad-news situation. Suppliers and clients share very limited degrees of separation. They know each other socially through family connections and religious, ethnic or political affiliations. And then there are those random neighbourhood acquaintanceships. People can be networked in multiple ways.

On the front end, a heavily networked business environment where "everyone knows everyone" is a wonderful advantage. That's the good-news element. Word-of-mouth rules the roost. We buy from people we know and know about. We value the referrals of friends to their friends; we give our business to the friends of friends. This is great for sales. But here comes the bad-news. The social codex is *toxic* for cash-recovery. Everybody's far too "close." Business owners are intimidated; they're afraid to chase their money. They're afraid to cross swords with their sister-in-law's brother's cousin-by-marriage or the high school boyfriend that the wife almost married but didn't! And what about riling the husband of your kid's math teacher or goosing a member of your elderly mother's evangelical church!

These may seem like facetious examples, but if you've ever had to recover cash in a networked sub-economy, you know from dreary personal experience they're not so far off the mark.

Thar's social risk in them thar hills!

It's very hard to perform the necessary pastdue tasks

when you're socially separate from your customers by only one or two degrees of social intimacy and always worried about giving offense. Being reasonable and logical, we might want to believe that customers will be more scrupulous in their payment habits, not less, because the social codex imposes a supplier-friendly payment discipline. We'd expect people to pay properly rather than aggravate suppliers they know personally, besmirching their reputations, social and commercial, in the process.

Of course, if we *really* believed any of that, we'd be donkeys out in the pasture! The social codex is a single-edge sword that cuts in favour of sales, not receivables. I can't tell you why that is, but it's a psychosocial truth. Far from fostering a world of socially careful payments, it has the reverse effect. The social onus falls on the creditor, not the guys and gals who owe the money. It's the vendor who's supposed to backoff.

Perhaps customers are thinking...

"My suppliers won't chase me too hard or too fast. I know them all, and they know me. That's why I can string them out for payment without worrying that they'll challenge me."

Okay, that's too on-the-nose. It's probably not that conscious or devious. Certainly not for most customers. But even as exaggeration, the point is accurate enough and should be taken to heart. Many customers seem to assume that only creditors should be socially reluctant in matters of money. Social reticence, they believe, should always work in *their* favour. And they're usually right when it comes to practice. Creditor ambivalence about "social" receivables runs deep. Suppliers worry about protecting their personal relationships and status. They fret about *negative* word-of-mouth and how it might cause existing customers to bolt while simultaneously preventing new ones from coming on-board.

"Chase me for money and just maybe I'll whisper bad things about you to everyone I know! And I know a lot of people that you know!"

Fact or fantasy, it's a what-if scenario that causes vendors loss of sleep. If it's happening to you, you know exactly what I'm getting at.

---

34. WITH FRIENDS LIKE THIS...

Let's game-out a "friendship" example:

The business owned by a very good friend of yours owes your company serious money. Maybe even crucial money. As the big cheese at the supplier company, the problem gets dropped on your desk. "Y.P., Mr. Owner! Your problem!"

Why you? Easy. Your A/R staff is nervous about going after your pal. They're leery of the consequences of pushing your bosom-buddy for payment. So you get to sip from the poisoned chalice, instead. "It's your company and your friend; you take care of it!" That's only fair, right? Well, in theory, yes. But again, not in practice. Here's why…

As you review the file, you begin to realize exactly what you're going to have to do to defend your receivable. You're going to have to lay it on the line with the delinquent company, risking personal and commercial damage to an important relationship. It's potentially disastrous. In fact, the whole prospect is so depressingly similar to chewing a mouthful of aluminum foil that you join your staff in donning the social reluctance straight-jacket. You won't make that call, *either*.

It's a humiliating and self-destructive climb-down. It's not in your business interests, and you know it. But rather than have that bumpy money-talk with a friend, you fold your hand. Result: corporate self-repression. You do nothing, except continue to worry. And what about "the other guy"? Does your friend-and-customer mind the impasse? It's not *his* impasse, is it? No one's pushing his buttons or crossing his boundaries. The status quo – non-payment – is *your* albatross, not his.

Do I sound unsympathetic? All right, it's true. Social risk *is* real. Yes, you might end up with a train-wreck on your hands if you chase social money the way you know you should. But it was a devil's bargain from the outset – and you climbed on-board. You benefited from the front end advantage of a networked environment; now you're in Risk Alley with an unpaid invoice.

As harsh as it sounds, it's a ground-zero commercial truth...

In business, there are suppliers and clients – but no "friends."

Anyone who does business with "friendship" as a supporting pillar of commercial activity is simultaneously taking a business risk and a friendship risk. And it's just not worth it. Far smarter and less painful in the long run...

Build a firewall between friends and commerce.

Vendors have to face life's social codes without giving social fear a default win. Every entrepreneur who's vulnerable to an intricately networked business landscape needs to realistically assess whether fear-of-consequences can be allowed to outweigh a real and present need for cash. It makes no sense to have to tell the trustee-in-bankruptcy overseeing the burial of your business that you let your company slip away to protect your social universe.

35. FEAR FACTOR

Social fear is just one example of fear. I've never worked in or for a company that wasn't, at some level and to some degree, afraid of its customers. It took me a long time to get my head around this. I understood *valuing* customers. I understood *respecting* customers. And I understood *serving* customers with pride and a sense of accomplishment. But *fearing* them? And especially those whose stock-in-trade is quarrelsomeness and habitual payment grief?! That I found both baffling and peculiar. Eventually, I got wise. All that free-floating fear, I realized, is rooted in the fear of *losing* customers.

Fear of customer loss is almost always an unexamined anxiety. And it's ubiquitous. That's because it originates in "salesthink," that conceptual black hole into which the common sense of many business people disappears without a trace. In Chapter 5, I uncloaked the essence of the salesthink problem. Let's revisit it:

What are the four conversations no business owner wants to have with customers? Sex, politics, religion and unpaid invoices.

At a recent small business workshop, the owner of a design company informed those in attendance that he never asks clients for payment, "no matter how pastdue they are or how much they owe." I was fascinated. (Okay, I was appalled, but I *acted* "fascinated.") I raised my hand and asked him what he was afraid of. Uncomfortable glances flashed around the room. Much squirming in seats. I'd hit the "fear" nerve. Everyone knew exactly what I meant. Salesthink kills.

To his credit, I suppose, the design company owner stuck to his guns; he was unapologetic. He said, completely without irony, that he didn't want to "destroy" his "sales relationships" by bringing up "the unpleasant topic." In other words, the topic of money – *his* money. It was ludicrous. And laughable. And sad. But many heads nodded in agreement. What his supporters heard was some pre-packaged mumbo-jumbo about careful "customer management." What I heard was the salesthink pledge-of-allegiance! Sales *above all else* and cash be damned!

Doesn't it seem preposterous for a business owner to "protect" his customer base by starving his own company of cash, especially considering that his non-paying customers aren't exactly worrying themselves to death over "protecting" that very same relationship? Isn't a good commercial relationship supposed to be is a two-way street? "What's sauce for the goose is sauce for the gander." Right? Apparently not for that designer – and too many others in that room, as well.

In a related situation, at an entrepreneurship convention I encountered the unhappy owner of a struggling catering company that had 7 customers on-the-lam. They owed him a total of nearly $20,000. Clearly, this was the kind of money the catering firm could ill-afford to abandon. A deep pit of debt for any small business with slim margins. When I asked what action he'd taken to jiggle the money tree, the caterer told me that his staff had been birddogging the unmagnificent seven "for over a year." Four had refused to communicate; the rest said they had no money.

I suggested that a year was at least twice as long a time-frame as any small or medium sized enterprise (SME) should tolerate in such circumstances, so perhaps it was high time to ramp up the pressure. "Try coercion." I said. "Threaten collection." The impoverished caterer just stared at me in dumbfounded horror. He couldn't do that, he protested. "I'll lose them as customers. I can't afford to let that happen." Huh?? What??

Education required. I pointed out that, after more than a year, these 7 deadbeats weren't "customers" but debtors and should be dealt with accordingly. But that wasn't what the gentleman wanted to hear. He'd convinced himself that he still had valid and valuable relationships with his 7 escape-artists. I couldn't move him on that point, so our discussion came to a thudding end. I made my way to the exit, shaking my head. Another salesthink casualty. P.S... that catering business has closed its doors.

Both examples – and I'm sure you can supply a few others –

amply illustrate how some business people genuinely believe that if they challenge slow-payers and no-payers, they'll force those relationships to a truth-or-consequences crisis and their customers will scat. Even if we accept that as a valid anxiety, we still have to ask *which* customers will do the scatting?

---

36. WHO JUMPS SHIP
(AND WHY)

Business success is measured by the strength
of a balance sheet, not the length of a client list.

There's a world of difference between losing good customers and losing bad ones. Good customers don't jump ship without reasonable cause – not if a vendor's products or services are desirable, prices are competitive, delivery is competent and staff is customer-friendly. And bad customers? Forget the contribution the baddies *seem* to make to the sales budget. Believing in spooks? That's more salesthink on-the-march. If their main "gift" to a vendor is a wad of unpaid invoices, these wearisome, predatory junk-clients are a liability, not an asset. Honestly, bad customers are like brain tumours. If we can cut them out, where's the loss?

So no more quaking in our shells, please. Say it with me now:

Bad customers be gone!

Got a few you'd like to disappear? Invite them to haunt the aging report of some other supplier, and believe me, that's exactly what they'll do. They'll move on down the track, burning-off supplier after supplier like there's no tomorrow.

The gulf between the good guys and the bad guys is a wide one, and it's occupied by a third force on your client list: the not-so-good customers – the NSGs. Everybody's got them; they're not in short supply. Not-so-goods exhibit poor payment habits, they're frequently found on vendors' "naughty" lists and some form of pastdue action is usually required to rein them in. Without that tug on the reins, most would just pay in their own sweet time, and that timing would not be very sweet from their suppliers' point of view.

If vendors don't chase, the not-so-goods don't hurry. So chase them we must. But is there really a well-founded risk of losing them just by trying to get paid? I say there isn't. Yes, a few NSGs may bridle and be on their way. It happens once in a blue moon. But try to see that as a blessing in disguise, not a calamity. Not-so-goods who dive overboard when pressed for payment are just proving that they're bad customers under their diapers. Be glad you found out sooner than later.

37. "NORMAL" MIGRAINE

A dangerous disease-of-thought permeates the business lives of entrepreneurs *resigned* to permanent cash flow "migraines" caused by poor receivables performance. They accept it all – the whole fireball of fiscal distress – as somehow "normal."

Business as usual? Par for the course? I don't think so! It's not that these companies won't pay for competent receivables supervision. It's not that they're afraid of their customers. And it's not that they know they're suffering but don't know what to do about it. Strange as it may sound, these enterprises are run by people who've failed to diagnose the source of their companies' "pain" because they accept "painful" as the normal way for business to be.

Whenever we encounter a company whose leadership thinks that constant A/R pain is natural, we know we're in "forgotten asset" country – the land of perpetual exposure to receivables risk. The inability to connect the dots from a scary aging report to an inventory of cash flow evils seems inconceivable, yet it happens. And when it does, it's hard to know what to say but…

"Awake! Arise! Smell the coffee that breweth on the stove!"

Sweating out payroll, tax obligations, rent, line of credit and loan repayments and becoming a regular fixture on the call lists of creditors will precipitate a chronic "migraine" no business should have to endure. Not if "cure" can be had by effective receivables control. If there's a king's ransom stranded in outstanding invoices and the searing pain of cash-crunch at every turn, entrepreneurs need to link those pieces of information like stray pieces of a jigsaw puzzle. The connection is causal…

Unrecovered cash = major pain and suffering.

That constant, thudding headache is an urgent warning of danger to company profitability – and even sustainability. Change is always possible, but change has to be launched by motivated leadership. It's not sufficient for businesses just to be in A/R pain. They need to be fully conscious of their pain and understand that there's absolutely nothing normal, inevitable or acceptable about living with it.

---

38. "NO, I DO *NOT* HAVE CANCER!"

Some business mavens don't realize that their companies have A/R "issues," mild *or* severe. They're unable to do anything positive about the problem because they don't see the problem – which is a problem in itself! Then there are the owners and executives who are acutely aware of poor performance in receivables but fail to act because they're unwilling to admit that their companies have *any* shortcomings, period. As if admitting that they're having problems rounding up cash is the commercial equivalent of admitting they have cancer. They're ashamed, scared, embarrassed and paralyzed. They're in deep denial, and denial never avails because unattended deficiencies just fester like opens sores that soon turn septic.

All businesses experience "issues" in one area or another. It's not a negative reflection on company competence or anyone's intelligence, and especially not when it comes to cash-recovery. Money is hard to corral; everyone's riding the same ranch when it comes to pastdue accounts. So we seize the day. We embrace the cash challenge and address that gap in A/R performance. It's an opportunity to do business better, and it's completely shame-free.

39. THE NO-MONEY MERRY-GO-ROUND

Suppose we run a widget-making company. We think we're successful at it. We seem to have good sales. People like our widgets; they keep buying them. But our company is steadily growing cash-poor because we can't reel-in receivables. Obviously, we need help – and we know it. But with declining cash inflow, the corporate wallet has tightened. Company leadership refuses to create a receivables position or hire an A/R consultant to manage the money-chase. "Can't afford it," they claim. So cash flow continues to spiral in the wrong direction. Much-needed "green" remains out on the playground with no playground monitor in sight. And round and round we all go on the No-Money Merry-Go-Round!

To call this a vicious circle is to say that the moon is airless. If a company's fundamental business problem is cash-crunch caused by too many unpaid invoices, then there's only one solution. Get those outstanding billings paid and get off the spinning disk of sorrow. That way, no one's going to be murmuring:

"Nice business. Shame about the receivables."

Cash-crunch ceases when we give neglected receivables the attention they deserve. If expert A/R skills are going to bring in serious money while costing us a mere fraction of what's recovered, then paying for that expertise is a good deal – and we can let go of that queasy, dizzy feeling for good.

40. MULE TIME

It's self-defeating and indefensible – that "mule" attitude of companies opposed "in principle" to the idea of spending cash to recover cash. They won't pay for receivables work, no matter what. Not outsourced, not in-house. They just bray at the sun and grow poor. *Hee-haw!* Who knew "principle" could be so thoroughly jackass! *Hee-haw!*

When I get this line of argument from an entrepreneur or V.P. Finance, I get cranky. I have to remind myself that, yes, there *really* are people who own or run SMEs but have little business education beyond their own commercial experience. They know their product or service; they know how to sell. But that's about it. Is ignorance a valid excuse? Not when a company's survival is poised on a knife's edge.

Stubbornness and stupidity is a costly way to do business badly.

Here are two donkey-tails for your consideration...

The owner of a media company approached me at a business networking breakfast. He'd heard about me from a third-party at his table and wanted me to know that "we should talk." "I'm all about change-management," he boasted. "I want to make changes in the way I do my receivables. You could be just the thing." So far so good. Except that every time I tried to follow-up and set an appointment with him, I got an excuse about why now was "not a good time."

Having the seen this "movie" before, I sent him an email that reminded him that he'd courted me, not the other way 'round. I told him I didn't plan to chase him for fun. Did he want to talk receivables or not? Within the week I was sitting in his office and getting the big showcase on how he did his receivables *personally*, how *no one* could ever do it better than him and he didn't see why he should pay *anyone* to manage his pastdue accounts!

Obviously, Mr. Change-Management had been abducted by aliens who left this guy in his place. *Hee-haw!*

Once upon an aging report, I was asked to visit a tabloid-format, twice-weekly community newspaper in Metro Toronto. You know the kind: a lot of pages of community happenings and a lot more pages of ads, ads, ads. Having spent 3 years in magazine receivables, I knew the ad-space drill quite well. This was a wagon I knew how to fix with my eyes closed.

I was graciously welcomed by a very worried publisher and an even more worried general manager. They really, really, really needed my help, they said. I didn't doubt them. Their fear had an odour, and it filled the room. We talked for 75 intense minutes, and during those 75 minutes, I was treated to full disclosure of a truly dismal situation. A shocking litany of multiple exposures to a vast array of non-paying advertisers. The percentage of over 90-day receivables was truly frightening. The actual dollar amount was monumental.

I wondered how all this was possible. Here was a go-to tabloid for community news in a self-described "world class" metropolis. The paper was widely distributed. The advertisers were numerous and diverse. And even a quick gloss of a single edition proved that there were no fly-by-nighters; in fact, many were local blue-chip types. Metro majors. So who the @%$^ was managing their receivables?! Clearly, no one.

I thought: "I don't get it. This is a business that should be raking it in hand over fist like a Vegas casino. Where's the problem?"

Then they told me "the problem" – and I understood immediately. The sales team was responsible for cash-recovery. *Hee-haw!* I'll have more to say about that in future chapters, but for now, let's stay with the moment...

I took the next 15 minutes to explain (a) why recovery by salespeople is a dubious proposition at the best of times, but (b) yes, I could create a receivables supervision regime that would maximize the recovery potential of the sales team. Publisher and G.M. were very excited by the prospect of rescue. But I sensed another emotion in the room: guilt. I felt it coming – and it came, alright! "This is just great," said the publisher, growing more red-faced by the second. "But there's a glitch. The paper's owners won't pay for A/R management." *Hee-haw! Hee-haw! Hee-haw!*

I sat there in silence. But I was thinking: "Do I look like a federally-registered charity to you?!" There was nothing I could do for them. Not on that basis. I declined their offer of contra ad-space – a lot of it – in lieu of real payment. I wished them good luck and walked out to the parking lot knowing that I'd just had 90 minutes' worth of school time at Muletime University.

Here's where I'm going with these two sad sack stories:

There's a reason why the budget of any formal business plan includes a line-item for A/R management. It's just good business. No commercial entity will ever see 100% of its receivables waltz through the door within the time allotted by credit terms. Chasing receivables is a natural and vital business duty. And since someone has to play the part of the good shepherd, that someone requires compensation. Paying for effective A/R supervision is a standard business expense. No more, no less.

Company owners who make it a point of pride never to pay for receivables efficiency are condemned to fourth-rate receivables results. It's hard to feel sorry for them. In my opinion, they're leaders fudging on their leadership mandate and hard to take seriously as captains of profitable enterprise. Their penny-wise-pound-foolish "principle" harms no one but themselves – and, of course, their companies and employees.

41. THE WRONG PEOPLE
FOR THE RIGHT JOB

Many business principals are clear on the importance of receivables supervision. They don't need to be convinced. They're aware that pastdue pursuit and cash-recovery aren't optional, not if their enterprises are going to deliver dollars and grow. They know all this, and yet they still get it wrong in practice. They're victims of Wrong People Syndrome.

For a variety of reasons, these owners and senior managers believe that press-ganging salespeople, receptionists, bookkeepers or sisters-in-law into pastdue work is effective, smart and cost-free. They're sorely misguided in their thinking. Human resources count when cash-recovery is on the menu. A/R supervision that gets the job done right requires the right person using the right methods. It takes training, experience, suitability and know-how. Owners who insist on assigning their receivables portfolios to inexperienced staffers who have no A/R aptitude, no recovery skills, little interest and less time aren't doing their companies any favours. They're treating cash as a low-priority, zero-cost, no-skills zone. That's three strikes right there: wrong, wrong and wrong.

Just who are "the wrong people for the right job"? Well, beyond those itemized in the previous paragraph, add the company G.M., and above all, the owners themselves. But let's start with the receptionist or sister-in-law...

Neither is likely to be effective, and for the obvious reasons: no toolbox, no background in receivables and probably the wrong temperament.

Your staff bookkeeper? Well, she has a bookkeeper's toolkit. That's a start. She's definitely in a position to understand your receivables issues. But will she have the time, the commitment or the right character? The same goes for an outsourced bookkeeper – with one important addition. Your external bookkeeper can't be expected to treat your receivables as a normal part of her job-description. Even if she takes on the pastdue challenge, she's more than justified in treating it as a menu extra and building additional charges into her fee structure. I certainly would.

Involving your salespeople in cash-chasing? Now, that's truly problematic – despite being far too common. Here's a commercial riddle to ponder:

Q: What do you get when you mix a sales mandate with cash-recovery obligations?

A: A counterproductive receivables strategy that undermines sales confidence and customer trust at the same time.

To me, this is one big lose-lose proposition, as we just saw in the "Mule Time" chapter. To maintain their sales personas and sell effectively, sellers avoid the bad-guy role of money-chaser like the plague. Can we blame them? Switching hats from sales-buddy to cash-cop and back again is an arduous, disorienting task. It confuses the salesperson; more significantly, it confuses the client. Salesmen and saleswomen need to be perceived as "the good-guys." They have to build simon-pure relationships of unalloyed positivity with their customers. But don't misunderstand. I'm not opposed to having salespeople tender wise advice about the handling of customers on my pastdue roster. In fact, I welcome it. I value the input. Salesfolk are usually pretty good judges of character; they know their clients. But experience has convinced me that muddying sales waters with the negatives of cash-recovery undermines salescraft and creates uncertainty in the minds of customers.

Please take these to heart:

• Is a customer whose account is pastdue more or less likely to take a salesperson's call if he thinks there might be a pay-up agenda instead of a selling agenda?

• If a salesperson shakes the money loose this time, when she calls the next time, hoping to make a new sale, what kind of comfort-level will she encounter on the other end of the line?

Salespeople are incentivized to sell. That's what we pay them to do, and that's what they do best. We don't offer them financial incentives to round up dollars; and even if we install a receivables commission structure to sweeten the pot, there may be nothing in the personality profiles of our valuable sales heroes to qualify them as experts in running down outstanding cash. Take me for example: I can round up dollars. I've lassoed millions, I suppose, over the course of 20 years. But please don't ask me to sell anything to anyone! I just don't have that talent. I'm a lousy salesman, and that's because selling goods or services and lassoing greenbacks are two separate aptitudes. Salespeople know this instinctively. And more power to 'em!

So...

Can a business that uses its sales specialists as internal collectors have a happy sales force as well as spot-on receivables performance?

Not that I've ever seen. Something's got to give in that muddled arrangement. Maybe it's sales damage. Maybe it's poor A/R outcomes. Perhaps it's the worst of both worlds.

My advice?

Don't pollute a salesperson's selling relationships with cash-recovery obligations.

This brings us to the heavy-hitters: the company G.M and its owners. Owner time and senior manager time are much too valuable for back end work. On a moment by moment basis, the big brains of any business create more value for the company via sales, marketing and promotion and R&D. They're front end folk by inclination, habit and experience. If they communicate directly with customers at all, there has to be a sales motivation and payoff. They should never embroil themselves in conversations about monies owed, except as a last resort. That is, before an account is sent to collection or a suit filed. Keeping "clean hands" allows business principals to ride into town as white knights ready to save the day.

The king never collects his own taxes.

As "king" of your commercial castle, stay "kingly" in your relationships with customers. You're far more useful to your firm as a relationship-fixer than a would-be collector.

Conclusion? Allow employees to stay in the roles for which they were hired – the ones at which they excel. You want someone with accounting designation doing your financial statements, not a chemical engineer. And having a medical degree isn't a useful qualification for being a head shipper. Receivables are no different. The right fit for the right job. That's the personnel equation that always works.

WHERE'S **MY CASH**?!

IT'S ABOUT
YOUR ATTITUDE

_____

42. THINKING YOUR WAY THROUGH IT

_____

As we've seen so far, successful receivables performance is the result of the confluence of skills, method and something I'll just call "the thought process" (for want of snappier terminology). By this I mean, how we think about our company's role as a supplier, how we think about our customers and how we think about the money we're owed but haven't yet received. If we don't conceptualize these components properly, if we can't formulate the right philosophy of credit and debt, creditor and debtor, then we won't be able to make the most of even the smartest set of A/R policies and procedures. And we'll waste the skill-sets of our best receivables staff.

As you go through this short pep talk on the attitudinal components of A/R management, consider your own attitudes. Look for new ways of thinking that will enhance your current payment prospects.

43. WHAT IT'S NOT

It's not astrophysics. It's not magic. And nobody gets strapped to a liquid-fuel rocket and fired into the stratosphere. Managing receivables is systematic office work, plain and simple. It requires structure, common sense, a way with people – and a thick skin never hurts. When you're dealing with customers and cash, things can get tangled and unpleasant from time to time. Human edges can be sharp. There are challenges, obstacles and extenuations in receivables, just as there are in any department. But the bumps, bounces and bruises are all manageable if a supplier company shows determination in defending its invoices.

Determination paves the royal road to payment.

44. DEFENDING YOUR RECEIVABLES

You're not always David. Your clients aren't always Goliath. And it's rarely a case of combat to the death in the desert. Nevertheless, it takes an act of will to make the right commitment to A/R management. Your business doesn't thrive unless you make a winning commitment to sales. Likewise, it won't prosper without the same degree of dedication to cash-recovery. When it comes to managing pastdue clients, a stone to the middle of the forehead at great velocity is probably a little brisk, but as a metaphor for the defense of commercial cash, there are worse ones.

---

45. RENOVATE YOUR ATTITUDE

There are no "naturals" when it comes to reading the riot act to customers who don't pay when they're supposed to. The ways and means of successful cash-recovery aren't immediately obvious or second-nature to everyone. Yet ways and means can be learned. And it's all about attitude. When an invoice has grown too old to ignore, we must *insist* on getting paid. Now, *that's* attitude – the kind I like! But suppliers sometimes get it wrong. Common sense takes a vacation, and when it does, vendors will hear themselves asking – and perhaps even *begging* – a delinquent customer for his cash. *His* cash?? Wait a minute! If we're owed money, exactly *whose* money are we talking about?

46. WHOSE MONEY IS IT, ANYWAY?

One of the first objectives in receivables consulting is to encourage business owners to ask:

"Whose money is it, anyway?!"

Remember Howard Beale, the outraged, unhinged news announcer in the 1976 film "Network"?

"I'm mad as hell and I'm not going to take it anymore!"

That's the one. Well, I want entrepreneurs all over Canada to go to their office windows, throw them wide-open and yell:

"Whose money is it?! It's mine, damn it, not yours! I want my money and I want it now!"

Okay, no, I don't *really* want anyone doing that in real life – but it's a good fantasy exercise. And that's because not being sure about whose money you're chasing is an attitude malfunction that desperately calls for a shift in a new direction.

When you've fulfilled your end of a supply bargain, when you've honoured a contract by delivering goods or services and dispatched an invoice, there's only one thing left to conclude the deal. You need a payment. And until you get that payment, what's actually happening? You're financing the purchase your client made from you! Good ol' Customer Bill is borrowing *your* money, and *you're* financing the involuntary "loan"!

Well, okay, perhaps you agreed to let Bill borrow your money interest-free for, say, the first 30 days. That's a normal commercial concession. But there is no shame, disgrace or attempted theft in asking a customer to pay when the time to pay has come. After all, it's not *his* money you're asking him for, is it? Morally and legally, you're entitled to expect payment according to the terms and conditions established in the papertrail. You're authorized to act in a deliberate and time-sensitive manner to retrieve your cash. So, tell Bill what's what and get paid!

---

47. JUST SAY "ADIOS" TO LITTLE BO PEEP

Like the clueless shepherd girl in the nursery rhyme, businesses content to leave their receivables alone, hoping they'll wander home of their own accord, are deluding themselves. What's that supplier inattentiveness all about? Could it be that smart, capable entrepreneurs who've built vibrant businesses really don't care about getting paid? I don't believe it, and neither, I'll wager, do you. So why in heaven's name do good businesses have bad receivables? In a majority of cases, it's just a lack of time for systematic pastdue follow-up. Or a deficit in human resources. Or a failure to install and follow policies and procedures that guarantee efficient, systematic cash-recovery. But I think there's also something else.

Whenever we scratch the surface of unproductive receivables, we're likely to find a patina of resistance and fatigue in the executive suite. Let's be honest. Being owed money puts an unwelcome psychological demand on all businesses. It's a demand to "do something." And it's disconcerting. Most of us aren't confrontational by nature. We don't like to challenge, demand, pursue, tussle, hector and aggravate. We prefer to sidestep hot-button moments. We want to be nice and have our customers be nice in return. Consequently, we tell ourselves expensive, delaying fairy stories that prevent us from acting energetically and confidently. Here's a potpourri:

- "I'm too busy to make that pastdue call today."
- "We're too nice to have good receivables. We don't know how to be nasty."
- "I don't know what to write in a pay-me-or-else email."
- "I don't how to handle a gimme-my-money phone call."
- "I'll give my customer another week to pony-up."
- "My bookkeeper will look into it next month"
- "I'll send a fax tomorrow. Maybe."

Yeah, right. Tomorrow – always tomorrow. Mañana, baby! Never today – like *right now, s.v.p.*!

Excuses abound and multiply over time. And what happens when the moment of reckoning is delayed into a sequence of tomorrows that never seem to arrive? Slow-payers whose intentions may be good but whose payment habits favour cash-hoarding aren't getting a prompt to pay. Unprompted, they remain disinclined and unmotivated to do what's needed. They dilly. They dally. They dawdle. They postpone. Remember, they have their own set of infinite tomorrows when it comes to making payments, and I'm not sure we can hold that against them. They have a cash agenda, too; they've got rotten receivables and A/P pressures to content with. Is it any wonder that they're telling themselves:

"If our suppliers don't seem to mind that we don't mail their cheque today, why should we mind?"

Round up those missing sheep! Please!

Slow payers aren't motivated unless we motivate them!

48. EBENEZER, THE
UNMOTIVATED CONTROLLER

One of my favourite business fables can be showcased right here...

Out there in the fractious world of commerce, there is a wise but unmotivated controller. Ebenezer by name. Why he's "unmotivated" you'll soon see, but he's a smartie, alright. Ebenezer's wisdom, which is pretty slippery, originates in the strategy he employs to make sure that cash owed to suppliers stays warehoused in his company's bank account. How does he do this? Read on...

The Unmotivated Controller is very resourceful: he also has nerves of steel. That's what you need to be a successful commercial miser. But Ebenezer also has a secret weapon. It's the one without which his plot to sequester vendor cash can't survive. As a public service to all suppliers, I'm going to blow this man's cover right here, right now. I'm going to make Ebenezer's secret weapon known to the commercial public, so it can never work again. Here it comes...

The Unmotivated Controller's secret weapon is... you.

Or perhaps I should say: your inaction.

If you're static with unpaid invoices, if you stand pat and avoid, if you play Bo Peep, that Supergirl of Carelessness, Ebenezer, the Unmotivated Controller, wins hands-down. Every time. Oh, you'll get paid – well, maybe you will – but it won't be according to your credit terms or cash flow needs. Ebenezer will call the cash shots, and he'll keep calling them until you get wise in return and take control of the payment tiller.

It shouldn't surprise you greatly to learn that our Unmotivated Controller is employed by Customer Bill. As we've already discovered, Bill's company pays only when Bill feels good'n'ready, not before. Although Bill's sleazy attitude permeates his enterprise, being an efficient, organized and dutiful C.A., Ebenezer has all 30-day payables well under control. Every invoice that should be paid as per credit terms is ready to go out the door. All cheques are cut, signed, enveloped and stamped. In fact, we'll spot them sitting right on the Ebenezer's old mahogany desk. And there they are! Take a gander…

Notice that they're in two neat but distinct piles. One pile is noticeably smaller than the other. These are the cheques that are going to be mailed by noon today. The envelopes in that second, larger pile aren't going out today. In fact, they're not going anywhere anytime soon. They're staying exactly where they are: on Ebenezer's old mahogany desk.

Where are your invoices in this set-up?

- If you're an *essential* creditor or you've *motivated* Bill's Controller with pastdue communications, your payments are in the pile that will be mailed today. You're going to get paid because you've said you *expect* to be paid – and by a specified date. You've insisted; you've defended your receivables. Or you're going to get paid because Bill doesn't dare mess with you. As an essential creditor, you can inflict explicit harm to Bill's operations if cash-recovery becomes too much of a struggle. He can't afford to alienate you.

  But...

- If you've done nothing to defend your receivables, if you've been sitting on your hands, if you've been unfocused about cash or just reluctant to "make waves," you're on-hold in the second pile. Your money will remain warehoused in Bill's corporate bank account till... Bo Peep's lambs wander home – which will be... well, we just don't know when, do we?

The moral of the Ebenezer story? Make waves when wave-making is needed. The Ebenezers of this world are very good at reading your intentions and *especially* your fears. If you intend to be paid, act accordingly. The most likely outcome is successful payment. If you do nothing, unmotivated customers and their parsimonious controllers will take the obvious inference and nothing will be its own reward.

Funny how that works.

We can learn to live with Ebenezer and his ilk because controllers and other "official" payment gatekeepers are basically businesslike employees of businesslike enterprises. They require motivation but usually only one round of it. In that respect, they're like most slow-payers. If suppliers are also businesslike and take positive action on pastdue invoices, then the unmotivated will take the hint, get motivated and Canada Post will do the rest. It's a big game, for sure. But it has a big rulebook. Use it.

49. MAKING THE OMELETTE

I'm sure you've heard it before. Maybe you've even said it yourself. Either way, it remains one of those platinum-plated truths about life – and that includes business life:

You have to break an egg to make an omelette!

Recovering your cash can be an omelette–making event. I'm not advocating breaking business relationships as a matter of course, but I am in favour of breaking the silence in matters of monies owed. Saying you expect to be paid is the place to start making a good cash breakfast.

Cash is The Breakfast Cache of Champions!

Last time I looked, success in a for-profit business is measured not by how many customers it has on a client list but by cash earned from doing business with *paying* customers. So pursuing your receivables doesn't make you a bad person. You won't get struck by a lightning bolt tossed javelin-like by the god who protects bad clients and habitual delinquents. And, no, you won't hate yourself in the morning. But you *are* more likely to get paid. And on your own terms.

Eggs Bankable, anyone?

WHERE'S **MY CASH**?!

THE CUSTOMER IS ALWAYS... THE CUSTOMER

50. CUSTOMER COMPLIANCE

I've already had a fair bit to say about customers and customer relations, and I'm not done yet. More to come in the second half of this book. Some key points will be restated for educational value; I like to make sure I hammer the nail flush to the board. And especially when it comes to the two diverse viewpoints found in most SMEs. There's the "customer" as seen through the eyes of your sales team, and there's the "customer" encountered by your receivables manager. The differences can be unsettling.

So…what do we want from our customers when it comes to cash-recovery? Compliance. And when do we want it? Now? Well, if it's pastdue cash, yes – definitely *now*. If it's not overdue, then we'll want it in sync with the terms of credit codified in the sales agreement. We've already established that there's always a significant percentage of clients who pay according to – or very close to – our credit terms. From that part of our customer base, nothing more can be asked, except repeat business. We just wish *every* client was on the same cooperative page. But, unfortunately, it's not like that, is it?

When we triage our client list on the basis of payment profile, we get the good, the not-so-good and the bad, and we shape the receivables action we take according to this three-way split. The good guys are self-managing. We let them do their thing. The bad are few in number – at least we hope so. We weed them out of the garden over time. And the not-so-goods are the ones we have to work on consistently. They're permanent managerial projects.

I'm not one of those who subscribe to the celebrated business bromide: "The customer is always right!" Sales-folk may think that way, but I don't. My commercial experience just doesn't bear it out. Too often, in fact, experience has proven the opposite, and I'm willing to bet that 99% of receivables managers will back me up. When you're on the receivables side of the blanket, the customer is frequently wrong – and sometimes spectacularly wrong! Some clients misunderstand the contracts they've signed or the nature of the product or service they've received. Others misread the invoices we send them. And still others – fortunately, very few – are just downright dishonest and dissembling in their bobbing and weaving over payment. That's why I believe that "the customer is always the customer" – but that's all. And absolutely when it comes to cash.

Leaving aside the contemporary obsession with share-holder value, customer satisfaction has always been front and centre as a customary and definitive measure of why-we're-in-business. Do our customers *matter*? Of course they do! They matter plenty – just so long as we're always cognizant of the supplier-client "power" question...

51. WHO TRAINS WHOM?

If you're a dog owner and a dog lover, you'll appreciate this "doggie" observation:

If your dog thinks you're the dog, you have a dog problem and a problem dog,

Oh-boy, that is *so* completely true! I'm dog-crazy, and I take life with my Goldens very seriously. But here's one thing I learned early on as a dog guy... When you raise a pup, life is much better for all concerned when your dog knows she's the dog and you're the human. Someone's got to be Alpha, and it better be you! Most dogs grasp this order-of-battle from the earliest hours of puppyhood. They're hardwired for the programme, but it needs to be reinforced by training. If you train your dog to be a good dog, the result is social happiness. If your dog is allowed to train you to accept doggie behaviour that works against a good relationship and a happy home, the result is grief – and an unhappy, unruly dog.

So it is with suppliers and clients in matters of cash. Different species, yes, but the same organizational and social behaviour. If this seems like a surprising and unflattering analogy, take a moment to reflect on it with specific customers and their payment habits in mind and I think you'll find it's actually fitting. When we engage in pastdue pursuit in a systematic manner, going through the motions week after week or month after month, we're telling our iffy, slow-paying clients that we expect our credit terms to be honoured. We're training them to expect to be called out on wayward payment habits and collared to accelerate cheques. What we're *not* doing is letting them train us – and for the simple reason that we *just can't afford it!* No way, no how. We need our cash now, not on the never-never or, worse, not at all.

Despite the tedium of facing down the same delinquents again and again, this methodical dunning does get results over time. Sometimes, those results arrive only because late-payers experience their own version of "pastdue fatigue." They get tired of our calls, faxes, emails. They get tired of showcasing the same excuses and evasions. Gradually, they begin to improve their days-aging. Incrementally, they become more manageable and less of a problem. In short, they comply.

In spite of our best efforts, however, some slow-payers may never be fully trained. They may never wiggle their way into our "good" books; they may never become the "net-30" payers we'd like them to be. Yet, many will eventually show the benefit of having been exposed to effective training. Perhaps they'll begin paying upon receipt of a first pastdue communication, instead of a second or a third. And some will mail their cheques just in time to reach us before we pick up the phone and make the first pay-me-now phone call. Doesn't sound like much? It is, if you're faced with dozens of delinquencies every month.

52. GOOD CUSTOMERS HAVE WINGS

Trisecting our client base into "good," "NSG" and "bad" just means we're prepared to be realistic about our customers. It's not prejudice; it's self-protection. We have to parse our customer list into descriptive categories that distinguish apples from oranges – and both from rotten tomatoes. As I keep repeating – because it *warrants* repeating – good customers are the backbone of every commercial enterprise. We sing their praises on-high. We want to grow our business by increasing their numbers. We shout it all over town:

"We want more good customers! A lot more!"

The good guys buy our goods and services, appreciate them, and they show their appreciation through their payment habits. They pay on time, and they also don't mess salespeople around on the front end. They sign their contracts and work orders without undue fuss. They provide positive word-of mouth; they don't hesitate to refer. They reorder when they have need, and they're quick to inform us in a frank, calm manner if we've missed the mark somehow in servicing their accounts. Good customers keep us on our toes and improve our businesses every day, in every way. So the very last thing we want to see is our vaunted "angels" slip their wings and take a tumble.

53. ...AND THEN THERE ARE THE OTHER GUYS

It's the not-so-goods where we focus most of our worry-time and worry-energy. We don't want to beat them up; we'd just like them to raise their payment game and pay their way off our "naughty" list. We won't give up on them; we'll keep nudging them in the "nice" direction, hoping they'll take the hint. Some will, some won't. *C'est la vie.*

And the out'n'out baddies? Can leopards change their spots? No, but maybe there's still a shred of hope for some of these commercial deviants who seem to delight in making us irritable. Maybe we'll get through to a few of them before we feel forced to cut them loose. Maybe they'll see the error of their bad-boy ways, even if they never become angelic partners in commerce. We can dream.

54. CUSTOMER INTIMACY

I'll forgive you if you suspect that "customer intimacy" and its kissin' cousin "the commercial hug" are just a little, well, lightweight. But let's be sure we're talking about the same things. We may love our best clients, but it's not the same kind of love we feel for our significant others, kids, parents, friends or pets. So when business consultants and organizational theorists talk about "customer intimacy," rest assured that the kind of intimacy they're thinking of isn't the same as the intimacy attempted on a moonless summer night at the local drive-in.

Getting close to your clients – or trying to – is an intelligent, self-interested strategy. Getting close can mean getting a better handle on the nature of your customer's business, the industry in which it operates, what its needs and challenges are, what its owners are afraid of. In other words, what makes the client clock go tick-tock-tick. Then there's the personal dimension. We cultivate personal relationships with our customers because business is often personal; it's about people. People do business with people they like and trust. Remember the hugely popular '80s TV series "Cheers"?

"Sometimes you want to go where everybody knows your name."

That nails it for business, too, not just downtown watering-holes. Given competitive pricing and equivalence in products and services, people will choose a new supplier or stay in the fold of an existing one on the basis of personal intangibles: acquaintanceship, comfortable communication, feeling understood, accepted and cared about. It may sound Pollyanna-ish, sure, but it's also reality. Take sales for example. Is there a salesperson anywhere who doesn't know that commercial intimacy works? Is there anyone who sells for a living who doesn't want to be on a "hi-Jane-hi-Joe" basis with a purchasing agent, property manager or anyone else who can ink a purchase agreement or sign-off on a service order? The personal touch is bread'n'butter for selling. But what about the back end of the sale-to-cash process? Isn't intimacy hard to come by when we're trying to come by cash?

When dealing with the obstinate customers you'd like to consign to the lower regions of Hades, yes, it's tough slogging. There aren't a lot of good, touchy-feely moments to be had. You can't expect a comfy hug from a pirate. And with good customers, there's no search for intimacy, period. There's no need to "search." Good customers have the right attitude already. Standard equipment. The quest for intimacy is challenging and necessary in equal measures, however, when dealing with NSGs. Since these are the clients who form the majority on a pastdue roll-call, here's where we really need to develop and maintain cordial relationships. Naturally, it's a difficult mission. A money-chaser has to apply varying (and sometimes amplifying) degrees of recovery pressure to get NSG attention trained on paying outstanding billings. It's hard to stay on completely affable terms while twirling the cash-recovery lasso, but it can be done. It's a test of our people-skills…

Keep it firm but friendly.
Rope the cash, but keep the customer.

That's the m.o. the members of the Money-Chasers Guild aspire to.

Still, on a client by client basis, a lot depends on a customer's corporate culture, its financial state and its respect for suppliers. Some NSGs will never be better customers than they are now because they don't want to be. While they may never go totally bad, they don't want to get "close," either. Intimacy, respect and collaboration – these values don't seem to rate too high in their template of supplier-client relations. They're wary and distant, probably because they know that when a supplier snuggles-up for a "hug" it means a cheque has to change hands, and that's not necessarily what they have in mind.

Most not-so-goods manifest poorer cash flow than poor intentions. They're habitually short of "the ready." In an effort to retain what cash they have, they cheat on payables. And when they do, we can bet the farm that they're suffering from substandard A/R capability. They're cash-starved victims of the boomerang effect:

Can't recover receivables; can't pay suppliers.

And that merely reinforces the importance of the maxim at the front of this book:

"If everybody pays, everybody gets paid."

55. THE INFORMATION DOOR

Paying the bills is part'n'parcel of a mutually-productive business relationship. Unfortunately, people who owe money aren't always thinking about how to preserve a valuable commercial connection. If money is tight, often the atmosphere around payment is, too.

Reduced cash; reduced oxygen. Declining patience and etiquette. They're feeling squeezed on all sides – and not a hug to be had. When customers are facing daunting cash flow pressures, they can be tense and defensive, so the additional twist we apply when we try to get invoices paid can lead to an unwanted dust-up and a relationship rupture. Under these conditions, intimacy is a longshot, but it's not Mission Impossible.

Successfully keeping the not-so-goods onside while standing firm about payment can be as uncomplicated as getting "friendly" with a customer's A/P clerk or controller. A positive professional relationship between vendor A/R and client A/P can facilitate payment predictability and improved, mutual understanding. And if it only opens the information door instead, then it's still well worth the effort. While that's not quite as sweet as opening the door to immediate payment, subsidiary information from an A/P insider is a good deal more than just second-best. In fact, it has its very own gold standard. Frequently, tactical information about payment – when it's coming, what's holding it up, who needs to be prodded – is a valuable precursor to pulling a cheque out of an envelope.

Open the information door whenever possible and walk on through!

56. EXEMPTED!

I hate it when this happens, but I'm going to have to contradict myself. What I said earlier about the "king" not collecting his own "taxes" is still true, but there's an amendment:

"X" marks the spot for exemptions and exceptions...

In recent years, I've begun to accept a commercial reality I don't particularly like or approve of. There are too many SME owners who experience the jitters at the thought of leaving 100% of pastdue management in the hands of an A/R staffer or consultant. They feel they *must* keep an ownership hand in the process; specific pastdue accounts weight heavily on their minds. I can offer these entrepreneurs a measure of calm, but doing that requires an invention.

While I still firmly believe that an entrepreneur is one of those "wrong people for the right job," I accept that there are certain customers and situations that may be too sensitive to be handled by lesser lights than the company *seigneur*. Sometimes best practices have to take a backseat to other vicissitudes. But it can't be a random process; there need to be groundrules. So I've developed a strategy that accommodates owner involvement. This strategy has a few names, depending upon where and how I apply it, but the two most common are the unimaginative but descriptive "Owner-Managed List" and "Exempted List."

What I don't want to encourage is the irrational jumpiness of an owner whose fear of clients causes him to undermine a best-practices A/R regime. And I definitely don't want to discover that he has a scroll-length list of customers he wishes to "protect" from pastdue pursuit. That's self-defeating. A large number of protected clients also means big, protected dollars. An owner-managed list can't become a way of not dealing with pastdue problems and a safe-house for exposure and risk. But if carefully policed, a *limited* list of exempted customers can be practical. The entrepreneur must invest real time and effort into getting those pastdue invoices paid. If he works the list, if he gets invoices "taken care of," then the strategy will be effective. On the other hand, if the list just grows month after month, that's a sign that a long, hard second-look at the configuration of the list is required.

There's no exact formula for how many accounts and pastdue dollars can be safely housed in an owner-managed list. Obviously, less is more. For example, if a supplier has 50 pastdue accounts, and the company owner wants to put 40 of them into an exclusionary file, we'll have evidence of an attitude problem: owner fear overwhelming company cash requirements. But 2 or 3 out of 50 – about 5%? That's not unreasonable or unworkable.

What kinds of accounts should be owner-managed? The answer to that may be as varied as the businesses that feel the need to create an exemption category. However, the classifications that immediately come to mind are "maritime":

- **the big fish** – customers that are essential to company survival because of their sales clout

- **the unhappy fish** – customers that have an already-identified dispute in need of resolution

- **the complex fish** – accounts that have serpentine characteristics and need special knowledge and handling

- **the personal fish** – F.O.B.s (friends of the boss) and other clients where personal relationships may be too close and too vulnerable

If proactively managed on a king-to-king basis, there's good reason to expect successful outcomes more often than not.

AN OUNCE
OF PREVENTION

57. WE'RE EXPOSED!

We sure are! You know, one of these days I'm going to stop chasing other people's cash for about six months and write a screenplay called "The Naked Supplier." The storyline? The chillingly familiar tale of businesses that provide goods and services with little more than prayer and a promise of payment. My script will be a drama, of course. But there's always the chance that it might turn out to be a business horror classic. Sundance, here I come!

Okay, I lied. I'm *not* going to write that script. It's been done. Everyone's seen that movie already. It's playing every day, in every way, in every sector of the commercial economy. And that's the downside inherent in running a business that extends credit: exposure.

Since a receivable is a billing whose payment has been postponed for a designated period of time, until it's paid, that payment is only a hypothesis. *Maybe* we'll get paid. We *suppose* we'll get paid. Technically, our companies are "exposed" for the value of *every unpaid invoice* they carry. Exposed to the possibility of payment failure. Exposed to a midnight visit from the Grim Reaper of Cash: bad debt.

What can we do about this condition of exposure? Get dressed! Put some clothes on and limit the nakedness. How do we do that? By managing credit effectively, by lassoing pastdue payments and by dumping bad clients.

---

58. THE EQUATION

Bad clients = bad debt.

In the world's "oldest profession," it's called "a bad date": a dangerous encounter during the course of a commercial transaction. While every business has its risks, most business "encounters" aren't usually this furtive or illicit. On the other hand, I doubt there are many readers who haven't had to deal with a "bad date" at least once in their business lives. In fact, if we were able to magically snoop the client rosters of every profit-seeking business in North America, we'd find that almost every supplier has its unfair share of bad clients and dark, doubtful accounts.

Should we decry and denounce the multiple evils of doing business with junk-clients? You bet we should! Pirates of commerce, every one! Junkmeisters come in various shapes and sizes, and all harbour a fleet of bad intentions or exhibit heart-stopping incompetence – as amply demonstrated by the wreck and ruin they leave in their wake. Bad clients take your goods, services, time, attention and money – and then head for the hills! Or they just hang around like a noxious whiff that won't go away. Like something that died in the walls.

The typical baddie doesn't pay at all, or he pays short or so incredibly late that invoices need walkers and oxygen due to old-age! Baddies are also given to mischief-making during sale and delivery. With them, nothing flows smoothly. Haggling is constant. Cooperation is minimal. Language grows purple. Why do we tolerate this knot of unpleasant, unrewarding losers that complicate our business lives? What are they doing on our client lists? More importantly, what do we *do* about it? If we can't bring them into line, if we can't achieve a civil, beneficial relationship, and above all, if we're never sure from one billing to the next whether or not we're going to see coverage, then aren't these the clients we can learn to live without?

No one is in business to flirt with risk trafficked by toxic deadbeats.

The liability quotient of bad customers is always too high. Even if our always-hungry sales-brain makes us believe we have to put up with their flaming hoops and nuisance behaviour to make a sale, what we should never willingly put up with is the bad debt risk they inflict.

59. BEWARE THE DEBT VAMPIRE!

It was a dark and stormy night – and then it got worse. A lot worse. The debt vampire came a-knock-knock-knocking on your company door! His appointed mission: to suck the life out of your enterprise and leave it on a morgue slab with those red, telltale neck marks. This is every business' worst nightmare: the customer who owes you so much money that if his ship hits an iceberg and heads to the bottom, your business is going straight to Davy Jones' Locker, too!

The debt vampire is any client to whom you've become dangerously exposed in an expanding programme of debt. Due to a combination of lax A/R supervision and sales overdrive, the vampire has been allowed to place a sequence of large receivables on your aging report, usually in rapid succession. Or perhaps it's just a single invoice with a titanic net amount. Then you find out that your friendly neighbourhood Dracula can't pay you. Nor can he pay anyone else. Are you well and truly done-for? Well, there's no coercion option, that's for sure. Pursuing your vampire legally – if his company is actually still operating, that is – will probably result in the collapse of his business and yours as well. Very scary! Oooooh!...

Any profit-conscious business that knowingly allows a questionable client or a known baddie to build a potentially fatal exposure probably has it coming. Harsh but true. Business life is tough enough without loading up the company shotgun and firing both barrels at your own head. On the other hand, the debt vampire isn't your typical bad-guy. Not as a rule. He doesn't fit the piratical profile. And that's the problem. You won't see him coming down the street with a marquee "V" branded into his forehead. In fact, you don't see him coming at all!

Mr. V. usually starts out as a good customer – often a *very* good customer. A customer you trust on account of business history, third-party referral or some personal connection. Maybe he's an F.O.B. Friend of the Boss. Yep, he's got *bona fides* aplenty. Then one day, everyone in town realizes that your much-valued client has joined the ranks of the financially undead. Who knew! Was it misfortune? Was it misadventure? No one intended things to turn out so… toothy.

Just one of these monster customers can leave any business cold-stone-dead. But it's not inevitable. The best stake-in-the-heart is prevention. We can prevent commercial vampirism with rigorous receivables oversight. We never let any customer get too far ahead on the debt curve, and we rely on prudent credit procedures at the point-of-sale.

60. THROUGH THE HEART

What's an ounce of prevention worth? A pound of cure, or so they say. So when the debt vampire comes a-calling, I say: don't wait; act first. Slaying the bloodsucker before he slays you is a very sensible idea. And the weapon of choice? Carefully-crafted, well-policed credit management practices.

Unless our businesses are large enough to have credit managers on-staff, prudently vetting customers and contracts, what do we really know about our present or prospective clients? Can we be sure of their commercial health? Do we have accurate intelligence on the state of their cash flow and their ability to pay what they've agreed to pay? If our wellbeing is dependent upon theirs, isn't it in our interests to practice good commercial hygiene, learning as much as we can along the way?

It's a question of due diligence. Naturally, we'll be a little less twitchy with existing customers who own a good track record. If they've been doing business with us happily for some time, we have empirical confidence in them. But what do we do with existing customers whose payment profile has never been much to write home about? And what about future customers we've never dealt with before? We don't know them from Adam. How can we be sure they're not serpents slithering around our little Garden of Eden?

In this section, controversy ratchets up with a discussion of (and advocacy for) credit management. While receivables management and credit management are different business modalities, the latter has a direct impact on the former. Credit management is a condom for sales. Safe, secure receivables are enhanced where credit management has a clear role to play and plays it well, and they're undermined when credit control is kept shackled to a wall in the company dungeon.

A/R security begins at the point-of-sale.

My A/R manager's playbook warns you that selling can never be totally open-ended and random, not when credit and risk are entwined. Selling is a highwire act. Balance depends on salescraft and the salesperson's judgment – with credit management employed as the safety-net below.

Credit control has a major impact on receivables generally and on excessive exposures and exposure to dodgy clients specifically. Well-oiled, it can prevent receivables altogether, and it will restrain the receivables it doesn't preclude. But please understand this: On the assembly-line that takes us from sale to cash, credit control is always a *front end* responsibility. It's an a *priori* feature of the sale process – the well-dredged channel through which all safe sales must flow.

Credit management as an A/R afterthought
is simply too late.

61. CREDIT – WHERE CREDIT IS DUE

Between them, credit management and sound sales judgment form a formidable barrier against deadzone exposures. We manage the landscape of deal-making competently when we make sure our sales force is watching the company's back, and by establishing rational, workable policies that determine how much credit can be given to which customers for how long and under what circumstances.

When considering a first-time customer, we should ask these credit control questions:

- Do we want this sales prospect to join our customer list?

- Is this company or individual going to be a balance sheet asset or liability?

- What kind of commercial history will we unearth if we do a little digging?

Even when the vetting procedure suggests that risk is low and opportunity high, our newbie will still be the subject of other credit-related questions:

- Will we impose a credit maximum and police it, even if it means refusing future product or service orders?

- What payment profile will we demand at the outset of the relationship?

- What payment profile will we be prepared to accept once our prospective client has proven dependable?

Unfortunately, not even the best designed credit control

can provide 100% immunity against bad clients or good ones that fall on hard times.

All commerce is risk and the assumption of that risk.

Any client can fall commercially "ill" and spread the "infection" to its suppliers. But in the same way that we install smoke alarms and CO_2 detectors outside our kids' bedrooms, credit management provides greater security by reducing the risk of entangling our businesses with undesirables posing as profit-generating opportunities.

Credit control helps us mitigate risk.

As we've seen in previous chapters, granting credit is discretionary. A supplier may offer very limited credit or no credit at all. Some fortunate vendors can require full payment at the time of sale or, alternatively, upon delivery. Their restrictive credit policies reduce their receivables.

Reduce receivables with front end payment and you reduce exposure and bad debt risk. Eliminate receivables altogether and risk melts away.

What?! Grant no credit? How many commercial enterprises are so privileged that they can demand on-the-nose payment without crippling sales? How many businesses are field leaders with products and services so desired that their customers will pay without hesitation at the point of sale or delivery? Sometimes a vendor really is the "only game in town." Their ball, their rules. Swaggerville. But that's exceptional. Most commercial enterprises find themselves compelled to grant credit because that's the nature of their industry. They didn't choose the repertoire; they just have to sing along with the rest of the choir. Dampening credit will only dampen sales – that's their big fear.

Credit management is also courage management.

Broadly speaking, there are four control compartments in effective credit management: credit applications, credit checking, credit limits and credit terms. They function cooperatively, and some detail about each is appropriate here.

Credit Applications

A credit application is an informative instrument, to say the least. But mom'n'pop shops, one-person micro-businesses and most small businesses will beg to differ about practicality. They're not wrong. They have small exposures to numerous clients, and they're likely to view the "credit app." as a cumbersome and contentious frill. They prefer to operate on word-of-mouth alone – the anecdotal buzz about prospective and current customers. And while the grapevine is generally dependable, it tends to whisper in generalities. How much nuts'n'bolts detail is it likely to provide? Not a whole lot. So small seller beware!

It's hard to imagine *any* large enterprise operating safely without a credit app. procedure. And the same is true for many medium-size businesses. They all make high-value sales and carry invoices with significant exposures and bad debt jeopardy. Suppliers in this category have an urgent need-to-know about the customers they're taking on. They're swimming in the deep end of the risk pool. They need hard information to sooth their risk concerns, and a newsy credit application meets that need, making it a tool of indisputable utility. A credit application can also state a supplier's credit terms and pastdue interest percentage. I support that, especially when it's coupled with a customer sign-off. It lays out the credit terrain from the outset, and that's never a bad thing.

At root, a credit app. is merely an information-harvester. It gathers basic but strategic data about a potential or existing customer. This information may not be valid forever and a day, but it's more thorough and reliable than grapevine chatter. But what specific information do we want to harvest and why? Let's deal with the "why" part first.

In conjunction with a formal credit report, a credit application provides "intel" that will help a supplier decide whether a client is likely to be a good, stable customer or an unattractive risk. It will also assist in setting credit limits and credit terms. And should the account fall pastdue, it may become crucial to the money-chase and recovery of rental property from sealed premises. Accurate business information can be the difference between cash-recovery and bad debt.

What information should a credit app. "reveal"? There's no uniform template since each industry or business sector requires specific forms of information. Here, however, are some of the fundamentals many suppliers may want to know:

- Operating name and contact information (address, telephone, fax, pager, email, etc.)

- Business type (e.g. proprietorship, partnership, corporation)

- Corporate identity, if any (e.g. an "incorporated" or "limited" entity with or without a corporate number)

- Head office contact information (if applicable)

- Landlord contact information (if the supplier has rental property on-site)

- Contact information of business principals

- Commercial references (names and contact details for two or three current vendors)

- Banking details (institution/branch contact information)

- An authorization clause that permits the supplier to contact listed references

- Dated signature of at least one company principal

I readily admit, it's a lot of information. At first blush, it might even strike you as "aggressive." So not surprisingly, the elephant in the credit app. room is resistance. Primarily, the resistance of the customer, but if you encounter opposition from your own sales force, don't be too surprised. All the more reason that a vendor company requiring an effective credit vetting tool should fashion a credit app. that's as realistic as possible with no unwarranted fishing trips.

Credit Checking

Running a credit check – that is, sourcing a credit report from Equifax *(www.equifax.ca)* or TransUnion *(www.transunion.ca)* – is an informative asset if it either eliminates or confirms doubts about a client's creditworthiness, etc. But it's not free, so not every company can afford to secure a report on every potential client, let alone existing ones. Nevertheless, it's money well-spent if you have nagging suspicions or need to corroborate the buzz on the street. A $50-$75 investment may save you from making an error in judgment that costs you thousands.

What can you learn from a credit report? Quite a lot,

as it happens. Example: accurate ownership information. It's always an unwelcome surprise to discover that
the folks that you *think* own the company you're doing
business with actually don't – and someone else does.
Someone you don't know. Someone you can't access.
That's pause for thought right there. Credit reports
deliver proven facts. Ownership is just one of them.
Contact information, payment profile, late payment
history, collection activity and court "events" are all
equally noteworthy.

Which warning signs, in particular, should attract your
attention?

- ✓ a profile of habitually late payments
- ✓ assignments to collection – especially those
  that remain unresolved
- ✓ a history of suits
- ✓ unsatisfied judgments and asset seizures

Is bad news in a credit report a deal-breaker? I know
this will sound like commercial heresy to some
ears, but...

Some sales just shouldn't happen.

There's at least one skeleton in every company's closet:
the-deal-we-wouldn't-have-done-if-we-only-knew-
then-what-we-know-now. We're all so much smarter
in hindsight, aren't we? The rearview mirror is always
crystal-clear. What's smarter than hindsight? Foresight.

"Forewarned is forearmed." A negative credit report should set off the fire alarm and protect us from taking on (or retaining) a customer who may be about to rob us blind or go stark, raving, madly out-of-business.

We want to mitigate risk, not take it to the church dance for a waltz and a lemonade.

Credit Limits

Suppose that the results of the credit application and credit report have been positive. A prospective client has just passed muster. We'll treat this new company as a reasonable risk. A normal risk. At this point, however, we still want to establish credit limits. Where's our exposure comfort zone? What's the maximum level of exposure we'll allow this newbie to build?

Credit limits are a commonsense construction based on reasonable risk-assessment. If our new customer is a small business or a new venture fresh out of the starting gate, we'll be more conservative than we would be with a blue chip manufacturer or a government agency. As a matter of policy, we might set, say, $10,000 as the ceiling for any unproven customer. Now, let's reintroduce our favourite straw man and aggravation artist, Customer Bill, and test it out.

Our aging report tells us that Customer Bill has 3 unpaid invoices totaling $9,900. But our sales manager announces that Bill's company has just faxed in another

$3,300 purchase order. The credit alarm flashes red. Our answer has to be "no." The credit bar is set at $10,000; Bill can't raise it to $13,200. If Bill's payment profile was superior, perhaps we'd be tempted to cut him some slack and let him tote that fourth invoice. But Bill's firm doesn't have much capital in the good faith bank. It's a trust issue. We're not certain about Bill's financial health, and we don't have a good feeling about him personally. We think he's a bit of chancer. So we inform our sales manager that he can't process the new order until Bill's company makes an exposure paydown. Bill's on "credit-hold." No one needs another debt monster lurking in the receivables ledger!

Credit terms

Our review of the aging report has unmasked an additional problem with Customer Bill's account. We just learned that he has a high balance: $9,900, but now we've realized that his account is also pastdue. Remember, Bill has agreed to net-30 credit terms; it's in the papertrail for each invoice. And since Bill's company never pays on time, once again, we'll have to hold his feet to the fire.

Definite terms of credit tell customers when we expect to be paid. There's no point in having them if we don't enforce them with pastdue pursuit.

This time around, Bill has a pair of unpaid invoices totaling $6,000. One is 9 days old; the other, 24 days.

They're both "current" because they fall within the credit grace-period. But Bill also has a 58-day old invoice at $3,900. It's nearly a full month in arrears. When our sales manager reads Bill his rights about credit limits, there'll also have to be some crisp discussion about his annoying disregard for our terms of credit.

62. THE WAR WITHIN: SALES VS. RECEIVABLES

That dreadful grinding sound filling my ears has just been traced to the gnashing teeth of the sales-loving owners and executives reading this book. They're going postal on account of the last chapter. They're just about to scream:

"Woolley, you jerk! Your kind of credit management will asphyxiate our sales budget and put our company 6-feet deep in the cold, hard ground!"

Ladies and gentlemen, let's not panic. I hear you. Kindly put down those ivory-handle letter-openers pointed at my chest, and in return for your self-control, I'll tell you what I know about "the war within."

Salespeople and money-chasers are *not* eternal adversaries in company structure. It's really not a daily kick-boxing match. But every business I've ever been associated with has experienced a certain degree of tension – call it "ingrained opposition" – between Sales and Accounts Receivable. Overall, these departments and their staffers share the same big-picture goals: the health and welfare of their company and the security of their jobs. All shoulders to the corporate wheel! But beyond that, their sectoral interests often diverge and they're often at loggerheads over policy and procedure – and who gets to set both.

This oppositionality is not inherently bad. The tension of opposites in any organization can be dynamic and take it to higher ground; dialectical "edge" can motivate. But this in-built potential for sales–receivables combat still has to be managed by company leadership. A skirmish here, a skirmish there. We can cope. But the outbreak of wholesale inter-departmental warfare is unacceptable. And what's source of the problem? The combatants have cartoon views of their opponents.

Here's the sales narrative:

"If policy-making is left entirely to the conservative, cash-protecting fantasies of receivables managers, our companies' sales potential will suffocate. Receivables

*managers are inherently pessimistic and untrusting;
they're totally different from the good-natured, optimistic,
people-loving salesmen and saleswomen who make every
effort to see business through rose-coloured glasses and
keep commerce swimming right along. Handed the reins
of enterprise, these anti-sales accounting types will
smother it in the name of 'risk management'."*

Fair enough. We "accounting types" *are* obsessed with defending cash. We're averse to exposure. We avoid longshot odds. We mitigate risk. It's all true. Even the accusation that we're pessimistic and not very trusting. And it's all because we're always wondering:

"How can this go wrong, and how badly wrong can it get?"

Okay, so it's not a rosy way to watch the passing parade. But it's our job to think that way – and to act accordingly. Somebody's got to. And when we do, we eyeball the Sales department with a healthy dose of skepticism. What do we see but...

*"...a cabal of restless, reckless hawkers'n'talkers who
are all too willing to drag any warm body through the
door, dress it up as a credible customer and cook up a deal
that delivers a sales commission. In terms of genuine risk
assessment, salespeople can't be trusted to act in the real
interests of the company because their self-interest –
commission – will always try to run the show."*

There's both candour and misunderstanding in

each perception. Both statements are true and also caricature. Each party wants to defend its turf and prerogatives. Salespeople assert the primacy of sales. Receivables managers promote the royalty of cash. But it's not a zero-sum game; it's a symbiosis. Each department needs the other. Sales and Accounts Receivable are the Commerce Twins separated at birth. They may jostle and rub, snipe and snitch and frequently grind each other's gears to the point of rage, but the company as a whole benefits from their twin-y dialogue and crafts wise policy based upon its output – even if that dialogue is sometimes less than genteel.

We have to all hold hands, sing "Kumbya," sway to the happy rhythm of common purpose and work for the greater good: company growth and stability. Amen to that, brothers and sisters of the Congregation of Profit! Sales managers have to appreciate that, at the end of the day, cash rules the roost. Always. Not the number of clients. Not market share. A balance sheet counts only dollars, so policies and procedures that enhance the role of cash are useful while those that violate the interests of cash are useless. End of argument. But we're all walking a two-way street, right? So, for their part, receivables managers must accept that commercial health depends on a strong, respected and confident sales force making muscular, profit-producing sales. And those sales can't be made without engaging risk. There's no cash to covet if sales aren't made, which is why risk management policy that tries to reduce risk to zero by stifling sales is beyond stupid – it's senseless!

As always, compromise makes the world go round. So all that nasty, uncivil cartooning aside, what's the actual impact of cautious credit policies on sales? Of the four components, there should be little disagreement from salespeople about credit limits or credit terms. Both are in widespread use in the commercial world.

Let's suppose we manufacture high-end, high-cost medical widgets and have a $100,000 credit limit for all first-time customers. Out of the blue, a major research hospital in Calgary has found us on the Net. The medical purchasing officer wants to buy $500,000 worth of widgets. A single, first-time buy. Holding this hospital to our $100,000 credit limit is going to cause heated discussion in our executive suite – as well it might. Some will be hungry to close the deal; others will fret about exceeding the credit limit by a dizzying 400%. And both factions will be right. A half-million dollar novice deal represents a sweat-inducing leap into risk while turning the hundred-grand boundary into a pillar of concrete will be a guaranteed deal-killer. What's the right outcome? Obviously, there's has to be room for stretch. Time for a reality-check...

Hoping to break the impasse, our on-the-ball controller has just run a credit report. She glides into the boardroom waving it like a winning lottery ticket. It proves beyond question that the prospective client in Calgary is a well-funded public institution with no history of payment default. No negatives of any kind. Verdict? The risk is deemed reasonable. The credit boundary expands – peacefully – on a one-time basis. Reason prevails. The sale is made.

When it comes to credit terms, pastdue is pastdue. In my office, that's a rule carved in limestone. On the other hand, I've managed receivables for too long to be a policy purist.

Some customers will always be "more equal" than others; some invoices will be "more pastdue" than others.

Inequity is another fact of business life. One size never fits all. Not even when it should. Certain customers will have to be pushed at Day 31. Others can be counted on absolutely to issue a cheque at 45 days. Still others are certain for 60. In other words, pastdue forbearance may be good politics rather than bad receivables. Sometimes, it makes sense to leave well enough alone – at least for a while – and let a reliable customer benefit from some *monitored* A/R slack. Pick your spots. Choose your battles. No cookie-cutter.

I stand with the A/R management teams of this world. I believe that if a supplier's credit terms are pragmatic, they should be upheld with a very limited number of fair-risk exceptions. But salesmen and saleswomen know their customers better than I do – or ever will, so Sales department input is always welcome in my world. Provided it's informed and cash-aware. If salespeople wish to lobby occasionally for "relaxed" receivables, then on a case by case basis, I have no beef with that.

(I'm a salesman's son; I respect the craft.) I'll expect them to be intelligent advocates for their clients; I'll expect them to employ cash-conscious reasoning. But I will listen attentively and try to find the golden mean, if there's one to be found.

Credit checks should be uncontroversial, except with respect to cost. I can't think of a single reason why any salesperson would object to the sourcing of a credit report on an untested or troubled customer. The same can't be said, however, for credit applications. This is where the rubber squeals against the road...

Securing a "credit app." occurs on the sales watch, but salespeople aren't generally elated by the prospect of having to "sell" a customer on an information harvest. They're busy trying to sell the upside of a product or service. Negatives can cancel out positives, so in the sales-focused mind, the credit application merely injects one more node of potential customer resistance into the sales moment. But does robust credit management *really* complicate robust selling? Yes and no.

Sellers don't want a potential sale encumbered by risk-mitigating "downers." You really can't fault them for feeling this way? Or can you? Did anyone say selling was *easy*? If it was, everyone would do it because everyone could. But selling is undoubtedly *not* easy. It's an art mastered by the few: the occult art of persuasion. And part of the artfulness of selling in a credit environment is coping with safeguards, even when they turn some clients flinty.

No one wants to burden salesfolk with deal-busting baggage. But by the same token, no supplier can afford to go out on a financial limb, sale after sale. I expect sellers to support credit control. I expect them to understand the reckoning behind a credit application and "sell" that reasoning to the client. How? Well, among other things, by appealing to the client's sense of fiscal caution. After all, many business-to-business customers are themselves suppliers of goods or services. They have customers of their own. They know the lay of the land where risk is concerned; they sense which way the winds blow when it comes to exposure. Salespeople have to appeal to that caution, achieve customer empathy with the vendor's position and obtain compliance with credit management tools.

And if a prospective customer balks at a credit application, whole or in part? It's up to the sales rep. to ask why and take notes. Maybe the client has a valid objection. Discussion can follow; compromise can be sought. When I'm wearing my credit manager's hat, I have to be open to that, and I am. But there's a world of difference between being open and being careless, so naturally, I view credit app. resisters with some mistrust. Absent a justified dispute with the process, I ask myself: "Okay, what's this prospective client trying to hide?"

Too many hours of every A/R manager's day are

devoted to tracking down delinquents who want to play hide'n'seek when it's time to pay. When I see a customer-to-be starting out the relationship in game-playing mode, I'm inclined to dig my heels in. "Begin as you mean to carry on," say the Brits. If a potential client is demonstrating resistance and non-cooperation at the outset, salespeople and receivables managers alike should worry that this behaviour predicts what's going to follow.

In the final analysis, if unvetted customers turn out to be deadbeats, salespeople derive no benefit. That's why they have every reason to support and promote reasonable credit strategies that reduce the risk of receivables failure. It's that "ounce of prevention" that tips the scales like a heavyweight.

WHERE'S **MY CASH**?!

TOOLS OF
THE TRADE

63. INVOICES ALSO GROW OLD

With the next three chapters, I'd like to concentrate on the invoice and its *paterfamilias*, the aging report. These are the two most important documents in an A/R manager's arsenal. Together, they tell that vivid and uncompromising story: who owes what to whom. Let's begin with the invoice...

I noted previously that comprehensive, timely billing is essential because invoices start aging from the billing date. The sooner they're in the mail or dispatched digitally, the sooner you'll get paid. At least, that's the expectation. But one way and another, late or early, the invoice has a weighty job. It codifies sale information in final form – and it does it all on a single page (usually). It's the first payment prompt a customer gets, and in a perfect world, it would be the *only* prompt we'd need.

We usually think of price as the primary component of an invoice – and that's true enough. It's where our eyeballs roam. It's the strategic feature. But it's not the only information an invoice can convey to a customer.

64. INVOICE MESSAGING

The invoicing function of your accounting software should allow you to "message" your customers in a variety of ways. You'll do the obvious, of course. The fundamentals. You'll marshal customer contact info, the product or service descriptions and the pricing components. All this data will available via the paper-trail your order-entry clerk receives from upstream in your company. She'll build it into the invoice. Standard practice. But there are other important messages.

I'm referring to the "other" details that emerge from a sale. Not every one of the categories that follow will apply to every transaction or to every supplier's operations. And much depends on whether a company provides a product or a service. But in general and in one combination or another, this messaging "six-pack" should find a home in every papertrail: credit terms, discounts, payment styles, pastdue interest, property title and return-item penalties.

✓ Credit Terms
We've already covered credit terms in some detail, but here's a brief recap of the essentials:

Credit terms define payment expectations based on a

client's credit management status. They also determine when an invoice becomes pastdue. Credit terms come in various formats: due-on-receipt, 7 days, 30 days, 45 days, etc. In essence, it's whatever a supplier deems best, based on an assessment of company cash flow needs, the terms offered by competitors, industry payment standards and the unique perils of customer relations. Whatever they may be, your preferred credit terms should be stated in the papertrail, beginning with the credit application and the sale agreement/service order.

Clearly stated credit terms help your customers become good payers. If you want clients to pay on-time, they need to know your payment expectations, starting at the point-of-sale. Later, they'll be reminded via invoice messaging that your credit terms are unchanged – the same conditions-of-sale to which they originally fixed their signatures.

✓ Discounts

Discounts are commonplace in various industries. The most typical discount formats are "2/10" and "2/15." A discount of 2% of the pre-tax billing may be deducted by the payer, provided payment is received within 10 or 15 days of the invoice date. If it costs 2% of receivable value to secure 98% payment within two weeks, that's a pretty fair deal. It's cash flow friendly, provided you export your invoices on-time.

A discount is a carrot. It's an incentive. The goal: to get customers to pay on a turnaround basis. Receive the invoice today; pay it tomorrow. It's a due-on-receipt strategy with a little sweetener, and it works. Many corporations, public institutions and government departments/subsidiaries have tripwire A/P policies. If a supplier offers a timeline discount, they *must* take it. On the other hand, anyone who's ever used a discount strategy knows the drawback. Customers will take the 2% – and remit late anyway!

✓ Payment Styles

There are many ways to pay an invoice. In the same way that a papertrail specifies credit terms and discounts, specific comments on payment style may also be included. For example, if you have designated payment arrangements already in place, it's a courtesy and a clarifier to show them in your invoicing. Suppose your customer has paid a 50% deposit. Your invoice should reflect that prepayment. Or if you debit a client's account electronically, or have a credit card authorization on-file, noting these payment provisions on your invoice will help prevent your customer's A/P department from cutting an unwanted cheque and incurring a double-payment.

Here's a list of payment styles. Do you use them in your business? Could they be helpful payment tools?

- contra
- barter
- no-charge (courtesy or compensation for error)
- partial pre-payment (at least equal to tax portion/s of invoice)
- with order: cash/Interac/cheque/credit card authorization
- on delivery: cash/Interac/cheque/credit card authorization
- electronic debit (PAPP/PAD – with or without credit terms)
- with credit terms: cash/Interac/cheque/credit card authorization

Please note that payments via bank draft, money order, certified cheque & credit card are "hardmoney" on a par with legal tender or Interac. But the credit card option can be a honey trap. Driving payments to credit card is a genuine convenience that customers appreciate, but there's a price to pay for that ease-of-use. Vendors, watch out for those pesky merchant fees! They can really add up – and painfully, too – if a large number of customers pay high-value invoices with plastic.

✓ Pastdue Interest

I'm fully in favour of citing pastdue penalty interest (aka "finance charges") in every credit app. and sales agreement, and restating it right through to the invoice. For every month that a customer has exceeded your credit terms, the pastdue penalty should come into play – *at least technically*. If discounts are the carrot, pastdue interest is the stick. Suppose your company claims pastdue interest @ 2% per month. That wouldn't be unusual. Do the math on a sizeable billing that's been pastdue for a year. It won't make you rich, but it's still significant money.

There are industries where finance charges are used routinely, and customers routinely pay those charges. But many businesses find that the regular use of pastdue interest is a make-work project for accounting clerks. First, they have to create a debit memo to add the penalty percentage to the customer account; then they have to make that penalty "go away" when the customer pays the invoice in full but refuses to pay the finance charge. Even when the charge is automatically applied, it still has to be manually eliminated. I know of one company that writes-off $20K a year in "declined" finance charges.

As far as I'm concerned, there's only one good reason for *saying* you'll charge pastdue interest and only one good reason for *actually* doing it. And that's the ability to use finance charges as an award escalator if you take a client to court. Suppose you sue Customer Bill under a small claims mandate. You can help defray some of the expense by applying pastdue interest to a judgment awarded in your favour. But it must be contractually established. If you don't have finance charges encoded in your flow of documents, you can still ask the court to award pre-judgment interest at a standard rate. You might get it. Or you might not.

Building a pastdue charge into your sales and service agreements serves as a failsafe. Why *not* do it when it can mean a little more dough for you and a little more "education" for deadbeats? It places your exclamation mark on a debtor's account.

✓ Property Title

If you rent goods, a property registration or "true-lease" contract will enable you to secure your company's property if it's seized from the premises of a failed client. A rent-to-own agreement, however, may prove dicey.

Imagine you're renting kitchen equipment to a sports bar that goes belly-up. Generally speaking, the landlord, property manager, bailiff and trustee-in-bankruptcy will honour your proof of ownership. Upon receipt of suitable verification, your equipment will be released. But the situation is less clear if you've sold the equipment on credit or inked a rent-to-own agreement. Even though the kitchen goods haven't been paid for yet, the landlord, property manager, bailiff and trustee may take a sudden, unfriendly turn. They may fight to retain the seized equipment, claiming that the debtor had legal title via possession and a history of partial-payment. Which would put you up the unnamable creek without a handy paddle!

To forestall this unhappy result, your papertrail should

state that the seller retains property title until *payment in-full* is received. This formula isn't magic; it's not an absolute guarantor. But in the majority of such cases, it may be the claim-check that helps you recover your stuff.

✓ Return-Item Penalties

NSF cheques and failed debits are infuriating time-wasters. Your bank charges you when a customer's payment flops. Take the hint. It's a good one. Initiate your own return-item policy.

Penalty warnings about payments that crash'n'burn should be expressed in a credit app. and the rest of the contractual paper flow. Impose a discretionary charge of $25 per return-item for a first offence and, if you're feeling strong, a $50 hit for all subsequent "payment malfunctions." The objective isn't the money you'll see; it's to dissuade sketchy clients from becoming "rubber merchants" at your expense. They need to know that bouncing their wares off the walls of your bank account is not okay. Your business is not a squash court.

As with the application of pastdue interest, however, vendors retain full discretion over when to *actually* charge a return-item penalty. The real value of the penalty policy is its stick-value. But showing the stick doesn't mean you're forced to whack someone with it. Most likely, you'll bill penalties only to truly trouble-some accounts. After all, a client whose payments are habitual duds has earned a slap. Phoney payments deserve vendor pushback.

In the event that you have to assign a debtor to collection or file small claims suit, don't hesitate to back-bill all applicable return-item penalty amounts lingering in the customer file. Whenever possible, raise the value of your claim and escalate jeopardy for the debtor. More jeopardy means more leverage. But let me offer a word of caution here. Because even good customers cough up a hairball every once in a while, your penalty policy needs to be flexible and prejudicial. Here, too, one size does not fit all.

Recap? Contractual clarity matters. Product/service descriptions and price plus tax are not enough. When applicable to your business, each "can" in the messaging six-pack should be installed in the papertrail, including the invoice.

65. LOST SECRETS OF THE AGING REPORT

Sounds intriguing, doesn't it? Unearthing ancient and esoteric business truths! Decoding the arcane mysteries of money! Awesome! Except that it's all totally bogus. There's only *one* secret to the aging report, and that's that there aren't *any* secrets, lost or otherwise. And that's the true beauty of it. The aging report is completely guileless and candid. It tells it like it is – *exactly* like it is! – in uncompromising, transparent black'n'white. No guff. No spin.

Your accounting software package offers you an aging report format. Print it weekly or print it daily – but print it and find out where your money is. Because that's what an aging report is for. It's a comprehensive receivables journal. A no-nonsense tally of your company's outstanding invoices and absent cash. An aging report will tell you how many invoices and how many customers are implicated in your pastdue landscape. It answers the title question of this book. And your A/R manager's chase-time will be determined by its data.

An aging report demonstrates all outstanding receivables in aged fields. The timeframes for those fields can be calibrated to suit your business rhythm, but the default field structure comprises four columns:

✓ In the first column: invoices 30 days old and under. (In businesses with "net-30" terms, this column houses invoices that are "current.")

✓ In the second column, 31-60 days. (Normal payment range.)

✓ In the third: 61-90. (Absolutely pastdue!)

✓ 91+ in the fourth. (*Unacceptably* pastdue!)

Column totals reveal how your money is distributed in time, and these totals may also be expressed as percentages of total receivables volume. Edifying stuff – and worrying, too, if a business operates without receivables competence. No lies are spun. So it takes some courage to face an aging report that tells those "inconvenient truths."

Let's say you operate with net-30 terms and you're looking at an aging report with a total of $1,000,000 in outstanding receivables. You've got this aging split to consider:

• 1-30 days: 50% @ $500,000
• 31-60 days: 20% @ $200,000

- 61-90 days: 20% @ $200,000
- 91+ days: 10% @ $100,000

The half-million dollars in the first column is current, which makes the other half-million technically past-due. 50% pastdue?? That's got to put a few crimps in your cash flow. All right, let's soften the jeopardy. Now, let's assume that in your industry the *actual* past-due marker is Day 61, not 31. That's a marker many an SME feels comfortable with because it's a realistic indicator in a competitive environment. In this 60-day scenario, only 30% of your receivable dollars – $300,000 – are pastdue at Day 61.

Who just said "only"?! Was that me?? I sure hope not, because having 30% of your receivables pastdue is not something you – or I – can blithely gloss. It's 30% of your money! And it's warehoused in bank accounts other than your own! That's not the end of it, either. Rolled into that $300,000 is a good chunk of your operating capital – money you need for payroll, payables, loan repayments, capital expenditures – *and* at least some of your potential profit, as well.

Let's develop this scenario… If each overdue invoice is a $1000 billing on a one-customer-one-invoice basis, your errant $300,000 represents a titanic 300 invoices tagged to 300 clients. Let me tell you, that's a lot of chase-work! An Everest of chase-work! Too much? Sure is! Okay, I'll reduce the impact by a factor of 10. That $300,000 now represents 30 clients and 30 invoices at

$10,000 apiece. The prospect for pursuit looks a little less mountainous. "Only" 30 accounts in this pastdue climb. But before we break out the champagne and do a little jig, let's remember that each situation represents a grievous exposure of ten-grand – and it's still a 30% receivables shortage overall! No time to lose! Get on your chase shoes! It's runnin' time!

As the repository of unpaid invoices, your aging report is a powerful diagnostic tool. Like a hospital patient's chart, it speaks volumes about your company's receivables health. And receivables health is one of the foremost indicators of whole-company wellbeing. So, stay healthy, please! Print an aging report today!

THE CHASE
IS ON!

66. SORRY, TIME'S UP!

When the time-spring finally jumps, propelling an invoice into the wrong column on your aging report, credit terms are at an end. Time's up. Time to *pay*-up.

The older an overdue receivable grows before you begin the process of reeling in the payment, the greater the downside risk. Receivables get stale if left on the shelf too long. They become incrementally more difficult to pursue successfully as they age, especially after 90 days. So when chasing dollars, sooner really is better than later. But where exactly *is* "pastdue"? I get asked this all the time, and it's always the same answer. It's where you decide it is. If your company's papertrail says that credit terms are net-30, then *officially*, a 31 day-old invoice is pastdue. And "pastdue" is a definite call-to-action. The meter is running. Time to recover your cash. But it's not always a perfect segue.

Pastdue action may not begin precisely
where credit terms end.

Your business may be lucky enough to operate in a 30-day payment industry. Or your firm may be an industry leader that can call the shots on payment time-frame. In either case, your receivables manager will be able to twirl the A/R lasso the moment credit terms expire without fear of driving customers off the ranch. If this is *really* your situation, you're sitting pretty. You're one of the dominants. You're the envy of millions far less fortunate than you.

But are you "sitting pretty"? Can you really rope-in 30-day payment without customer fallout? While there are always a few king-of-the-hill companies, most businesses feel constrained when it comes to pastdue accounts. They don't have cavalier options. Your business is probably one of these. And if so, you've got plenty of company. To borrow a hockey analogy, you're a "grinder." You grind out market share "in the corners." That's why you're thinking:

"I can't lower the boom on my customers at 31 days. That would be suicide."

I won't second-guess you on that. In fact, I agree. Beginning the chase at 31 days could be a customer relations disaster. In addition to facing negative customer reaction, it's also a numbers problem. If your business has a lush client base and produces a rich crop of invoices every month, a 31-day fishing net will catch way too many fish. Too many pastdue billings to process without a few A/R staffers to work the load. So where will you set your *real* pastdue redline? Perhaps 45-days will prove more practical. Maybe 60-days is the safer option.

As soon as an invoice is *functionally* pastdue, a supplier has alternatives to choose from. Pastdue supervision can be performed by in-house receivables staff or by a receivables consultant working on-contract. I've referred to this mode of A/R supervision as the "recovery" model. In addition to cash-recovery in-house, you've got two external options: factoring and collection.

---

67. RECOVERY

As a receivables manager, my sympathies lie with the recovery option. I prefer to see A/R management left in the hands of a staffer or a consultant rather than shopped-out to a "third party." Pastdue pursuit is what happens *within* the walls of a supplier's office. And what's the goal? To turn a receivable, which is one kind of accounting asset, into cash – the *best* kind of accounting asset. A receivable on an aging report may have cash potential, but payment is the real deal. When billings exceed their designated terms of credit, they cross the pastdue threshold and recovery procedures begin.

A vendor takes action to recover receivable cash with two main aims:

✓ to secure full payment as soon as possible
✓ to maintain the supplier-client relationship

Good recovery procedures capture outstanding cash and reinforce commercial relationships at the same time. When a receivables manager engages in recovery action, she's determined to remove an unpaid invoice from an aging report with full payment. But she also wants to keep the client on-board for future sales. Customer retention is an integral part of the profit cycle. We prospect, sell, deliver, get paid and sell again.

68. COLLECTION – WHEN NECESSARY

On more than one occasion, I've asked a business owner what he/she does about pastdue accounts and been told:

"Eventually, we just write them off."

Now, that's a jaw-dropper in my line of work. The idea of doing absolutely nothing proactive about unpaid invoices before passively consigning them to bad debt is, well… I get vertigo just thinking about it! Can entrepreneurs really be so clued-out about the ways and means of chasing-the-money? Apparently, some can.

Another eyebrow-raiser? Assigning pastdue accounts to collection without an "inside" chase. That's one more poor excuse for receivables strategy. I have many good things to say about collection agencies, as you already know. But as a first-stop "remedy" for a garden-variety receivable, a collection assignment is premature – and no remedy at all.

Collection if necessary, but not necessarily collection.

Collection is the external method of debtor discipline – after all in-house efforts have gone south due to a lack of client cooperation. When we feel there's just no hope of maintaining a workable, paying relationship, we'll ask a collection specialist to intervene and "shake the money tree" on our behalf. Good for us!

Collection is a big gun, and sometimes we need a big gun in our corner of the battlefield. But untimely or gratuitous use of collection services is self-injuring in two ways. First, it's throwing away money on commissions. Who can afford to give away 25% of invoice value on a first-stop basis! And especially if it's cash we might have recovered ourselves with a little in-house effort. Secondly, it's political. A collection agency has no interest in the past, present or future of any supplier-client relationship. It's not what they "do," and it's unreasonable to expect otherwise. A collection assignment stuffs a customer into a cannon barrel and blasts him over the horizon, never to be seen again. That's all well and good when we've run out of patience with a proven loser. Lose the loser, by all means. But it's devastating to our client list when inflicted on everyday slow-payers. Let's not go there. Please.

69. FACTORING

"Factoring" under-90-day receivables means selling them to an external, collecting entity at a discount. How does it work? A supplier that's either in need of immediate cash flow or unwilling to chase volume receivables in-house opts to "factor" unpaid invoices. In return, the seller receives discounted payment from the factoring company. The typical discount range is 1.5% to 6%. In effect, that's the factor's fee. The higher the receivables value factored, the lower the discount, so most SME's can expect to find themselves on the higher end of the discount scale.

A factor shells-out in two stages. There's a substantial payment upon buying the invoicing, but paying out the remainder will depend on the factor's collection success with the receivables it's acquired. Factoring firms aren't in business to buy junk-receivables. They won't purchase a vendor's bad debt, so collectability counts in the factoring proposition. Any supplier that expects to see full payout can't use its factoring house as a dumpster for doubtful accounts.

While it should be noted that this isn't the only factoring model going, it's the most common one. Does it have application and value? Yes, within limits. It's a cash "solution" that works for some enterprises in certain sectors and circumstances. But I don't like the optics. Instead of being the reasonable A/R strategy of a fundamentally healthy company that plans to be in business today *and* tomorrow, factoring always feels like a receivables fire sale saturated with the odour of desperation.

Factoring and collection both hive off a percentage of a receivable. But because collection agencies take their commission upon receipt of debtor payment and remit the balance to the supplier, the receivable never changes hands. Legally, it remains the supplier's debt, so a vendor always some degree of input into how clients are being dealt with by the agency's collectors. But when a factoring house buys receivables, it deals with seller's clients as it sees fit. Now what does that say about customer relations?

And that's not the only problem. A supplier that sells its receivables risks signaling its clients that the business is in emergency mode. Is that the impression we want to convey? If customers sense a Titanic replay, they'll fret bigtime about the solidity of the relationship. They'll shop around for another source of service/supply as a hedge against a sinking. And the same goes for the vendor's suppliers. What are they supposed to assume? That a supplier selling receivables has fatally struck a cash flow iceberg.

Even if these are overheated assumptions and don't reflect a vendor's true cash conditions, perception is everything. Stark speculation, whether right or wrong, can undermine the confidence of all concerned, including the seller's employees. In fact, only competitors will be happy. They'll hope the decision to factor receivables predicts a door-closing sale.

70. MINDING THE STORE

Effective receivables supervision tells your customers that someone's minding the cash store. It says you're awake and cash-conscious, not fast asleep with your eyes open. You know exactly who owes, how much they owe and when payment is due.

When you review an aging report in search of pastdue targets, you identify those customers with invoices that have exceeded the terms of credit. The chase is on! And each pastdue file is kept active and worked *regularly* and *systematically* until conclusion.

The protocol of any pastdue procedure follows this 4-stage sequence:

✓ When credit time has elapsed, an unpaid invoice is pastdue.

✓ A recovery file is opened for each pastdue account.

✓ Pastdue clients are notified of the details of arrears with payment requested by a specified date.

✓ The chase continues until there's a definite conclusion: payment, settlement, write-off, external assignment (i.e. collection) or litigation.

71. HELLO OUT THERE!

Your A/R manager has acquainted himself with the details of a pastdue invoice. Next step: create the yoo-hoo moment. Time to communicate with the customer-in-arrears in a clear and effective manner. No lectures, no rancour, no bullying. Just the facts:

✓ the invoice number, date and amount
✓ product/service description
✓ purchase order/contract number (if any)
✓ payment options
✓ pay-by date

When it comes to pastdue procedures, I use a three-strike rule. Unless I discover something that makes me rush a file into collection or court, or turn it back to company ownership for review, I'll give every pastdue customer three chances to remedy a non-payment situation. Why three? Isn't one sufficient? Ideally, yes. In the real world, no.

Impatience is no virtue in receivables. I want to be sure that every slow-payer or no-payer who genuinely wants to come to the payment table can do so. I don't want to give up prematurely on anyone who'll pay with a little extra "encouragement." I keep it simple; I try to make it easy. As easy as the situation will allow. My goal is finessing payment not fighting wars. Still, my patience and my forbearance have limits. I'll dance with a delinquent for only so long. That's because every past-due dance means time and money to my employer. So if there's no payment and no substantive communication after three good will attempts, I'm not going to lose a wink of sleep over sending the file into a third-party environment. My conscience will be untroubled.

72. HOLD THE PHONE!

My first pitch in the cash-recovery process is almost always a print pitch. Experience has taught me to prefer systematic mailing, emailing or faxing of *primary* past-due notifications over Mr. Bell's excellent invention. I learned long ago that pastdue outcomes improve, and business relationships are less likely to get holed, when the phone *isn't* the first pastdue measure.

What's my beef with the blower? Phoning has many commercial virtues, no question. From the point of view of chasing money, two of the best are immediacy and directness. And let's not forget low cost. Yes, the phone works nicely on many levels, and it's definitely the first-use tool of many a business person in search of a cheque. It just doesn't happen to be mine. When it comes to a pastdue yoo-hoo, I'm all about tactics and content. Speed and access offer style-points, but they don't outweigh the need for strategic delivery of content. That's where the written word is the uncontested winner.

Primary contact about a pastdue invoice is about one thing and one thing only: a declaration about monies owed. I communicate pertinent pastdue information. That's my content, my agenda. A very deliberate construct. I have a money problem to solve; I'm a rainmaker who has to make it rain cash. To do that effectively, I have to successfully convey details about debt. I thumbnail the pastdue problem; I mandate the solution. Bing, bang, boom.

Because I'm "the voice of the money," my agenda has to be a demand. It's a *soft* demand, polite and businesslike, but it's *not* dialogue or negotiation. I'm not interested in discussion. Not just yet. I want my agenda to be complied with like a court subpoena, but first I want it *received and understood*. The written word is the perfect conveyance for the purpose because it's the ideal pastdue monologue. And that's the nub of the phone issue right there. Mr. Bell's "horn" is not an instrument of monologue (unless you deliberately arrange to leave voicemail – which I sometimes do).

When I reach for the handset and punch-in the number of a delinquent, I'm seeking *dialogue*. The phone gives me exactly that; it brings me into engagement with "the other." And that's just spot-on for the times I want to *interact* with the Customer Bills of this world. But it's not so great when I want to *unilaterally* state the facts. The moment I have to account for that "other," I have to adjust my agenda for whatever he or she is sending down the telephone line in *my* direction. I have to cope with a second voice. My focus and message may be diluted or diverted – even subverted – by that voice. Crosstalk just confuses the issue. Can't use it. Don't want it.

When I convey my chase agenda in print, it's under my complete control. It's addressed to the specific individual or department I want to reach, and it says exactly what I want it to say. I don't have to worry about the ambience of the moment or the mood of the recipient. I don't need to cope with a knee-jerk reaction and other forms of blah-blah. My agenda is there in lively black'n'white: an unambiguous directive about the payment cooperation I need on behalf of my employer. And that's not all. Once my print agenda has been received, it can't be *un*-received. Moreover, I have a copy of it. And if it's faxed or expedited, I also have proof-of-delivery. More certainty. More fodder for the papertrail.

My agenda is always about command-and-control. Who commands and who's in control? When a customer doesn't pay, she's in the driver's seat. Withholding money is a form of power. When I chase the money, I change the power equation. *I* take the driver's seat, and I use *my* roadmap for the trip. I take and keep control. In the vocabulary of chess, I insist on playing White.

I make the first move, and I retain the initiative throughout the process.

Here, again, are the command-and-control negatives of a first-pitch phone call:

- I can't be sure that I'm going to make contact with the person or department I need to speak with.

- I may have to leave a message, and that message will not accommodate my full pastdue agenda. At best, I'll deliver a précis. This précis will lack the professional force of print, and I'll have no way of knowing whether the message will be received by the intended party.

- Even if I make a connection with the right party, I can't be sure that it's a good time for a potentially difficult cold-call discussion about money. I have no knowledge of the disposition of the moment. I have no idea what kind of day that person is having and what his or her mood is. What if it's one of those legendary "bad days"? Not a ripe opportunity for plain speaking and clear understanding.

- If it's a bad day, it can get worse. There's always risk of explosion. Taken by surprise, the recipient of an unexpected dunning call may become testy, resistant, hostile. If things go boom, not only have I failed to convey my agenda, the whole process has gotten off on the wrong foot. I'm that much further away from banking a payment, and that's not where I want to be.

- Even though the conversation may be bump-free, I still can't be sure that my contact has understood the full pastdue agenda or taken appropriate notes about the details.

73. IN LIVELY BLACK'N'WHITE

That's me and my chase agenda climbing out of the envelope. Print first, phone later.

Nomenclature... Whether we call it a "pastdue notice" or a "late-payment reminder" is a matter of personal taste – and strategy. Some people prefer a heading that announces: "payment now due" or "payment reminder." The language seems less confrontational. Makes sense to me. Coming on too strong right off the bat isn't helpful; resolute is good, aggressive isn't. All we really need here is a clear, concise and businesslike yoo-hoo. We want it to show a little design skill and look clean and professional. And we want it on a single letterhead page without a lot of unnecessary, diverting text. Nothing that will clutter up the payment-needed message. And nothing that gives customers a reason to turn feral.

Typically, I attach the reprinted invoice and/or a current customer statement to a late-payment notice. Some of my clients think that's too fiddly, too fussy or just an added paper cost, but I find it useful because it's effective. It's graphic; it's unmistakable. In addition, if the company I'm working for accepts phoned-in credit card payments, I also include a payment-by-plastic memo. Something eye-catching that promotes card payment as a quick and painless get-it-done option. Anything that successfully persuades successfully makes the grade.

Perhaps you're wondering: "Why send the invoice again?"

- Invoices really *do* get "lost in the mail" – occasionally.

- Despite being delivered to the target company, an invoice may never get to the individual who greenlights payment.

- Even when it lands on the right desk, it can still get mishandled, mislaid or shelved before being approved and coded for payment. (This is especially true in large companies with a lot of internal routing or a firm with a high rate of staff turnover.)

When the invoice is re-sent as a standard part of a pastdue package, it puts an exclamation point on the payment demand. It also prevents a customer from claiming that the invoice has never been received.

Why send a statement of account? To achieve a two-birds-one-stone effect. Think of it as a payment-training tool. When you send a customer statement that displays current billings as well as an overdue invoice, your delinquent client may make amends by writing a cheque that covers pastdue *and* current items. If so, you've just gotten ahead of the payment curve.

The time component of any pastdue notice is a critical element. I'm referring to the pay-by date. Sending a pay-up reminder that doesn't include a specified paydate is like mailing a letter without a stamp. Doesn't do the job.

Suppose we harvest pastdue targets at 45 days. We're going to cherry-pick every 45-day invoice (or older) from the aging report. Every customer with a past-due invoice will receive a payment prompt, and each notice will bear a pay-by date. We have to establish that paydate, but on what basis? Let's use the fingers'n'toes method…

Notices sent by regular mail have to account for postal time on both ends of the journey: notice out, cheque in. Let's assume that most of our pastdue targets are local (i.e. in and around our own city and the general region). Say postal time is 3 days maximum, one-way. That's 3 days outbound and 3 days inbound. Six transit days. Now let's add 4 days grace-time so customers operating in good faith can generate cheques and drop them into mailboxes. That's 10 days in all, and that's our timeframe. If we prepare and mail our pastdue notices on the 15th of the month, they'll show the 25th as the payment-due date. We'll diarize that in our pastdue journal. We'll list every pastdue customer that needs to get a call on or shortly after the 25th if there's been no payment or substantive communication by that date.

That's the mail-out scenario. When faxing, emailing or expediting by courier or express mail, the outbound time is shortened because delivery is accelerated. We can allot a single outbound day for fax and email and two for expedited methods. But the inbound time for a cheque doesn't change. 999 times out of 1,000, it's going to be by regular mail. So, instead of a 10-day timeline for receipt of payment, we pare it down to 8 and diarize follow-up for Day 8 – the 23rd of the month.

74. CALLING FOR CASH

We're allowing time for written notification to take effect. We're on the lookout for a payment from each slow-pay/no-pay target. If we get paid, all well and good. Getting paid closes the invoice. No need to follow-up. Equally obvious is what has to happen when there's no payment and no substantive response. We're going to have to hash it out by phone. But what if we receive contact *without* payment? This happens often enough. A few days after sending out a fleet of pastdue notices, calls, faxes and emails start coming in. What do they say? Are we being offered a payment commitment? If so, is it full payment with a definite near-future date? Perhaps it's a protest over being called on the payment carpet. Maybe it's just a request for a return phone call.

Any response to a pastdue notice is a good response.

What's "good" about it? A customer that owes money is responding to our pastdue agenda. That's *very* good. Regardless of the content of that response, two important things have happened. First, the delinquent now knows what's on the table – and *we* know that the delinquent knows. Our pastdue document has done its job; notification has hit the target. Secondly, the client's response, positive or negative, is going to lead us to a next step in the process. We won't be standing still, waiting. And whatever that next step may be, we're going to remain in the driver's seat, keeping the chase bus on the road.

Payment is better than chatter. No argument. Yet, all experienced receivables managers know that chatter today is often a lubricant for payment tomorrow. Communication with a debtor is "something" rather than "nothing." It has substance and shape, however minimal, manipulative or combative. New information will surely emerge, and if we follow that information like a winding river, it may just lead us to voluntary payment in the not-too-distant future. On the other hand, it can also tell us we're spinning our wheels. We may discover that, for one reason or another, payment prospects have darkened. That's not good news, but it's more news than we had to work with before, and knowing it reorients our thinking, possibly pointing us in the direction of coercion. At least now we know where we stand; we can take the appropriate action. We know how to proceed and when to do it. We've achieved certainty, and we have conversation to thank for that.

If a notified customer doesn't make contact, it's down to you. Yes, it's finally phone-time! Unfortunately, it would take an entire alternative book to investigate the types of flowchart conversations that comprise a money-chaser's phone encounters with the chased. Those weeds are thick and deep, and this is not the time or place to try to snorkel through them. But we can still outline the main brushstrokes of telephone strategy.

Whether we're replying to the response of a past-due customer or calling a delinquent that's ignored a payment-due notice, what we want are answers to a pair of fundamental questions:

- *Question 1: "Are you going to pay what you owe?"*

- *Question 2: "When and how are you going to make that payment?"*

Nothing open-ended here. Question 1 is almost always a simple "yes" or "no" proposition. Failure to answer decisively usually defaults to "no." Question 2 ensures that there's substance to the first answer – something measurable and verifiable. A satisfactory answer to Question 1 is incomplete without a satisfactory answer to Question 2.

In most cases, we're going to get the kind of response we're after. We'll get a commitment to a specific amount and a payment date. After that, it's a matter of policing our customer's follow-through. A promise made may not be a promise honoured. But what about no-payers who say "no" to Question 1 or prove evasive on Question 2? If they're just not motivated to cooperate, then it's our job to supply the missing motivation, always keeping in mind that while we can motivate someone who won't pay, it's a good deal harder to motivate someone who *can't* pay. Knowing the difference is decisive, as we'll see in Chapter 78.

75. RAINMAKING

The money-chaser's job is to make it rain cheques, credit card debits, even contra. Under normal circumstances, the person we want to talk to about "the weather" is an Accounts Payable staffer, a staff bookkeeper, the controller, a financial officer or, in the case of mom'n'pop businesses, the *Grand Fromage:* the owner. And because we're still working our agenda, the first thing we do after we say "hello" and indicate who we are is to reference our pastdue memo:

"I'm following-up on my payment notice of the August 15th, regarding Invoice 1234 at $5,555.00."

That's it, that's all. How come? As proficient rainmakers, we can cut to the proverbial chase because we've *already* identified the A/R problem in the pastdue notice. That's why we sent that memo in the first place – so we could use verbal shorthand during telephone time.

And because we did it that way, our slow-payer *already* knows the score when we call. There's no great need to elaborate. No start from page-one. The issue is on the table. The mechanics of the solution are what we want addressed in this phone call, and we're focused on getting the right answers. We ask...

- ...whether or not a cheque has been issued, and if so, when it was mailed and what the cheque number is

  or

- ...if no payment has been issued yet, when will it be issued

We need a firm commitment plus commitment details. We want to hear *exactly* what we can expect and when to expect it. That is, unless there's a persuasive and credible game-changer. What would that be? News that significantly alters our perception of the facts. For example, we may learn that...

- ...the invoice has never been logged as a payable because it's in dispute; the person with greenlight authority has refused to authorize payment

- ...the individual who ordered the product or service is no longer with the company; no one wants to accept responsibility for a payment sign-off

- …their bank account is frozen

- …there's a bankruptcy proposal in the works

- …there's been a change in ownership

- …there's a trustee/receiver running the business

- …a bailiff has taken control of the premises

In each case, we've heard pertinent news that changes our understanding of the situation and sends us off in a new direction. Our thinking has been recalibrated; our recovery agenda undergoes retooling to adapt to changed conditions. But because true game-changers happen only occasionally, what we're more likely to hear from unmotivated customers are these juicy rhubarbs:

- "Oh, you"ll get paid. I just don't know when. I'll get in touch when I have a run date and a payment confirmation."

- "Our CEO is our sole signing authority, and he's in the Cayman Islands. I don't know when he's coming back, and I can't issue any cheques till he does."

- "You mean you didn't receive our cheque? I mailed it a month ago or more. It'll take me a week or so to dig out the cheque number and mailing date. I'll have to call you back."

- "We ran out of cheques and haven't received a new batch yet. The bank says they're lost and we'll have to reorder. It's going to take another two weeks."

- "We can't pay you until our pastdue client pays us, and right now he's not even returning our calls. You'll have to wait for as long as it takes for us to get our money."

This list of excuses, red-herrings, diversionary tactics and outright lies could be a lot longer. I could fatten it with 20 years of the kind of fatuous nonsense every receivables manager has to work through daily. But when we grind down to the bare bones, in each case this is what we're really being told:

- No. Go away.
  or
- Not right now. Go away for a while.

Whether it's: "Yes, we have no bananas," or "*Mañana, Senor*," what's happening here is a form of no-pay goaltending. Our pastdue agenda is being deflected, delayed or we have a customer who wants *their* receivables problem to become *our* receivables problem. Result? In each instance, our first phone call has amplified our concern that a receivable is at risk. And that's just call #1. Needless to say, it doesn't end there.

We're *not* "going away" and we're *not* going to meekly accept chatter about other companies' A/R difficulties in lieu of legal tender. Our money-chase ends only when there's a full or a settled payment or when the delinquent is verifiably out of business, without assets and beyond the reach of litigation. A non-compliant debtor should expect more calls, and more paper, before our pastdue file is finally closed.

---

76. DON'T DESIST, PERSIST

Before we turn the next corner, delving a little deeper into the chess match between supplier and delinquent, I want to address an important part of the pastdue chase: consistent and persistent follow-up.

When we quit on a payment, we're complicit in enhancing risk – the risk that payment will never happen.

Vendors who are stretched for staff-time never assign enough of it to receivables. That's because there's just not enough staff or staff-hours to go 'round, so A/R is frequently the last piglet at the time-trough – and with the customary outcome. Companies in this position are losing sight of the need to stay on top of each and every pastdue file. Sending out a pastdue notice or making a please-pay phone call but not following up for a month or two or more will bring home no bacon.

Systematic receivables follow-up is a best-practice, so stay the course. Persist, don't desist.

It's not about being a pest. There's no value in out-and-out harassment. But we're after payment *deeds*, not just payment *words*. So even though you've sent a pastdue reminder and made a follow-up phone call that seemed promising, sometimes that doesn't seal it tight. A few customers are going to be perpetually evasive or downright weasely. They have no immediate plans to cut you a cheque, no matter what they said during your call. They just told you what you wanted to hear. They're hoping you'll be satisfied with that. Maybe you'll go away for a while. Maybe you'll lose track – or lose interest.

Most customers who don't pay after telling you they would aren't actually bad apples. Many are poor apples. They'd pay if they could, but they can't. Others are just distracted apples. They're disorganized to the core and incapable of living up to a commitment to a precise pay-date. Whatever their category, they're still past-due. Nothing's changed. We can't just let them off the hook after a single chat that's proved inconclusive or insufficient. We have to be tenacious, and that means phoning, faxing or emailing again and again – usually once a week, at first, but perhaps daily if the situation takes on an urgent hue. No matter what, we stick with the chase.

77. INTO A CORNER

I'm not much of a chess player in real life, but I like using the chessboard metaphor to explain my strategic view of the chase for cash. I'll come back to this in a few paragraphs, but first I want to clarify my chase expectations. What do I want to hear when I make a pastdue call? One of the following:

- ✓ Payment has been sent –
  and I'm given specific details.
- ✓ Payment will be sent –
  and I'm given specific details.
- ✓ The customer is disputing the invoice
  and explains why.
- ✓ The customer is unable to pay.
- ✓ The customer is refusing to pay without
  credible cause.

In each of these scenarios, my pastdue agenda has received a specific response. In the first two cases, I'll monitor the arrival of the promised payment and get back in the saddle, lasso in hand, if it doesn't show up. With a disputed billing and an unhappy customer, the issue lands on someone else's desk – a sales manager, a quality-control supervisor, an executive in a corner suite. That "someone else" has to investigate and resolve the dispute if it's valid. A customer with a confirmed dispute will be asked to pay an adjusted invoice, or perhaps the billing will be written-off altogether (see Chapter 85 for further discussion).

You may be wondering why I'd *want* to hear that a customer is refusing to pay without justification? Because there's no uncertainty anymore. We're at end-game. The customer that *won't* pay is a *debtor*. I don't have a lot of recovery options, so I threaten to coerce and, if necessary, follow through on that threat. My duty roster slims by one account; my collectors-of-choice gain a new account. And just for the record, "I can't pay" doesn't justify non-payment; it's merely context. Even if I'm sympathetic to a customer's fiscal plight, and I always am – it's a damn hard world out there! – I can't give personal payment absolution. That's not my job or my prerogative. Within a yes-cash or no-cash framework, can't-pay and won't-pay aren't substantially different. The cash outcome is the same, even if the interpersonal perspective isn't.

As you've detected by now, I like certainty. I hunt for certainty. Certainty means I now know one of the following:

- A payment is forthcoming.
- A dispute is under review.
- I'm going to prepare third-party assignment or court case.

Certainty turns my crank and moves my yardsticks. What I don't put up with is sheer guesswork, extended not-knowing and the elongation of the cash-chase towards an infinite horizon. That's just too time-consuming, and time is one thing an A/R manager never has enough of.

So many delinquents, so little time!

And on that hurried note, let's resume the chessboard analogy by resurrecting our favourite delay-artist, Customer Bill...

When I've got Billy-Boy in the pastdue crosshairs, I put him on my mental chessboard: that situation-room in my head. Where Bill's concerned, my entire money-chasing agenda, whether in print or conversation, is designed to cut down his escape-routes on this imaginary platform. Bill is a troublemaker; Bill traffics in delay. This is already well-established. I need to eliminate his incessant ducking and deaking, his weaving and bobbing, the hiding'n'seeking – all that evasive hopscotch from square to square that Bill uses to keep me off-balance.

What do I do? I track him down in a methodical and

deliberate manner, reducing his access to open spaces on the board. I want Bill trapped in one of the four corners with nowhere else to go, because when I finally catch up with him on that corner square, Bill has to face a truth-or-consequences choice. Either he deals fairly and negotiates payment or he's off my board entirely. And if I knock Bill off my board, I'll watch him tumble down, down, down to the collection woodshed or a court date.

"So long, Bill! It's been miserable knowin' ya!"

Think I'm too militant? I don't. I have too large a case-load of pastdue accounts, with more waiting in the wings, to play silly-buggers with an evasive, unproductive payment-resister. Especially when there are other slow-payers who *will* come to the payment table if I yank them along behind me like Gulliver towing Blefuscu's navy. My time is my employer's money. It's my responsibility to prevent delinquents like Bill from eating up the A/R management clock.

78. TRY A LITTLE TENDERNESS

Having taken a hard line on won't-pay customers, I've probably given you the impression I'm a ruthless, cash-clawing dictator. Not so. I'm a guy with feelings who searches for heart-and-mind balance when facing the can't-pay narrative. So let me make this point perfectly clear:

Not every pastdue event is, or has to be,
a cash-chasing blitzkrieg.

I don't want to give anyone the idea that receivables management is all-extreme-all-the-time. It's not actually a blood-sport. Most customers with overdue invoices will require some kind of reel-in process, yes. Some will extend that process for a round or two before doing what's needed. But only a few – and a very few at that – will actually force a truly hard-edged encounter.

As a general rule of engagement, there's more
shepherding than shelling in cash-recovery work.

I try to be mindful of the fact that every pastdue customer is an individual case with a unique narrative, history and relationship. And there are always going to be times when customers that you trust and respect are unable to make definite and immediate payment arrangements. When that happens, easy does it. A little sympathy now can prevent a lot of remorse later. In the immortal words of Otis Redding:

"Try a little tenderness."

Pedal-to-the-metal pursuit is counterproductive if applied to the wrong targets. When finally revealed, those "extenuating circumstances" causing non-payment can make the over-zealous money-chaser look very foolish for ridin' into town with guns a-blazin' and his brain a'-sleepin'.

Look before you leap. (Or end up in a heap.)

I've learned this lesson the hard way – and on more occasions than I care to admit. I've pounced on the prey – and fallen flat on my face. Oh, those "extenuating circumstances"! The fact is, people take vacations. They have illnesses and homelife troubles that pull their focus away from business. Companies have physical plant disasters: floods, fires, structural failures. And of course, good customers run into bad cash problems. There are many reasons why a valued client abruptly becomes a pastdue concern. Some of them are tragic; some may seem outlandish. But they all require a little sympathy and forbearance. At the outset, at least. To cite just one example that came up recently in my own work life: death...

The Dark Angel doesn't respect commerce any more

than any other field of human endeavour, so a death has a heavy impact on any business, whether it's a dead king or a dead spear-carrier. It's a 2 x 4 across the back of the head. For a time, everything's topsy-turvy. The room spins. There's personal grieving, corporate mourning and sometimes a dangerous loss of institutional memory. It takes time to replace a key staffer and get the successor up to speed. If a proprietor or a capital partner passes away, a will has to be sorted out. Sometimes there are probate issues. And then there are the pressing questions of succession and company direction. The admiral has left the bridge of his flagship forever. It's a sad, chaotic and worrying time for all.

In my own case, as soon as I realized the company I was chasing was bereaved of its V.P. of Administration, I knew I had to take a giant step back and re-develop a strategy-with-a-heart. Which I did. Luckily, I hadn't gone into the process looking for a punch-up, so I didn't have to make an embarrassing retreat. I was able to offer sincere condolences, rather than sincere apologies for being an uninformed, tactless schmuck – and it was duly noted and sincerely appreciated. My client received a nice thank-you letter in response and we held a feelgood parade around the company kitchen, knowing we'd had a near-miss!

Practise "cash-karma" and be generous in spirit.
Show short-term patience; win long-term dividends.

Not every unclear pastdue scenario is a game of "chicken"

that requires chessboarding. The customer who's in arrears is not always trying to cheat you or make you blink first. If you find yourself facing those "special circumstances," just swallow hard, offer sympathy and receivables slack – and hope for a cash-bearing outcome somewhere down the road. Profit-seeking can take a day-off once in a while; you'll survive. You may go unpaid in the short run, but you've shown human decency, and good customers always remember that.

79. THAT GAME OF "CHICKEN"

Notwithstanding Mr. Redding's "tenderness" mantra, it's hard to be a commercial saint. No supplier can afford the luxury of carrying too many hobbling accounts at any one time or for any length of time. Of course, hobblers inhabit every supplier's client base, and regrettably, so do the "chickenizers." Two very different species, however. Hobblers inspire our sympathy; chickenizers make us homicidal.

Chickenizers are those congenitally bad customers that

play the irritating game of payment "chicken." It's a test of wills. Who's afraid of whom? Who's going to do the training and who's going to be the dog? Who's going to fold their cards first? It's exasperating!

It's not that chickenizers *can't* pay. Maybe they can; maybe they can't. That's just the point. You're never sure about their real intentions and abilities. And that's just the way they like it. Being in control.

"What you don't know can't hurt me!"

That's the chickenizer motto. What you *do* know, however, is what you finally realize after a few fruitless circuits around the mulberry bush. This is just the way they operate. It's the m.o. they employ to hold onto your cash for as long as they can. Chickenizers like using your money, if they can get away with it. They like its interest-free conditions. In fact, they're the very best borrowers in your inadvertent lender programme – the one you didn't even know you had because, well, you see, you're not actually a banker!

Playing business chicken requires plenty of chutzpah and stamina. Chickenizers have both in spades. They're prepared to be harassed, aggravated, threatened and dissed – just as long as their suppliers never actually do anything that's *dangerous* to their wellbeing. Chickenizers want their creditors in the deep-freeze – frozen in futility. Chasing is A-okay, as far as they're concerned. Fax, phone, email, whine, moralize and threaten all you like. They're impervious to righteous indignation and bilious protest. Vendors can huff'n'puff till the sun burns out; chickenizers keep right on "borrowing" their money.

"Chase on, Mr. Supplier! Catch me if you can!"

Maybe it's a kind of sociopathy. It makes the chickenizer feel powerful to be the centre of your attention and the object of your frustration. Just so long as he keeps that game going, going, going…

"I dare you to fire me, Mr. Supplier!
I double-dog-dare you to coerce me!"

This is chickenizer brinksmanship talking. You're at the very heart of the game now. The chickenizer's going to take it to the limit; he's going to take *you* to the limit. And keep you off-balance. You'll think you're in Wonderland with Alice. For instance, he'll suddenly start talking up a good story about payment tomorrow or payment next week. Never payment today. He'll have you wondering…

"Maybe he'll pay if I do it his way and wait a little
longer. But if I try to push the pastdue envelope, perhaps
I'll lose him for good and then I'll never get paid!"

Uncertainty and indecision. Is that what you're feeling, Mr./Ms. Supplier? Then it's working. You're under the influence of a barnyard fowl and your buttons are being pushed. You've been *chickenized!* Happily, there's an exit. You *can* end the game without losing it or walking away humiliated and disgruntled. How? Stop playing. Start coercing.

Seize control! Ramp up the jeopardy! Chickenizers aren't stupid. It's their game; they know when it's run its course. Unless they're busted flat, the moment you begin playing hardball may be the very moment they pay-up as if nothing had ever been amiss. It's mystifying. That is, until you begin thinking like they think. Chickenizers are outlaws. If you don't set good behaviour boundaries for them, they certainly won't set any for themselves.

Do chickenizers always pay in the end? No, but it's not unusual to find a chickenizer writing a cheque when he knows the string is played out. Sometimes, you'll get paid after sending a registered or expedited letter that outlines an "or else" plan for collection or court. Or from time to time, a chickenizer will chick-enize his way into a collection situation. Then your collection agency gets a cheque after making a first collection call – and you're out 25% of the receivable's value! Insufferable! Some chickenizers will even delay all the way to small claims court, hoping to force an advantageous settlement at a mediation conference or a sawoff at trial. That's another characteristic of the breed: a love for nickle'n'dime "victories." They're infuriating stinkers, alright. But they're inventive. Gotta give 'em that much.

80. PLAYING HARDBALL

I just mentioned "hardball." That's a baseball metaphor well-entrenched in contemporary vocabulary; it doesn't need definition. But it does need some limits when we're talking about its commercial applications.

When taking pastdue action, you want your A/R manager to be adroit. You want her to finesse payment to the best of her ability. No one wants to make every single unpaid invoice a battle-royal. On the other hand, if all her nice-girl strategies go nowhere because a delinquent isn't sufficiently motivated to comply, you can't be afraid to let your money-chaser throw a fastball. High, hard and inside.

If you're forced to play rough, then play smart while you're at it.

We all want to make the most of customer care and client relations. That's our first instinct, and it's the right one. But sometimes we need to send an unmistakable message across the plate. We want uncooperative clients to recognize the limits of our patience and our readiness to defend our receivables. We draw that "line in the sand" for all to see. And when a customer crosses that line, who's to blame for deterioration of the relationship? Think about it. Your non-paying client, that infamous chiseler, Customer Bill, has eaten your lunch and walked away from your counter. He's had the benefit of your goods or services and failed to pay. Maybe he's made payment commitments that never transpired; perhaps he's even stiffed you with bogus cheques. Who's the bad guy here? Bill or you? I can tell you in no uncertain terms: *It's not you*. So wind-up and deliver that horsehide!

81. NO BARKING ALLOWED

But none of *this*, please. I mean the fang-brigade. Even when dealing with problematic customers, pastdue procedures still have to be civil. Civility works. You'll catch more flies with sugar than you will with s**t. So no snarling permitted.

Hanging tough over money, which is good, doesn't sanction being unprofessional, which is *not* good. Aggression-right-out-of-the-gate is disastrous. It's bad A/R practice. It demonstrates a lack of commercial understanding, and it doesn't advance the cheque-writing process one nanosecond. Losing-it emotionally, even with constant aggravators, is also out-of-line. When you're irate and yelling your lungs out, you can't think strategically and you're not listening carefully. An emotional blowout may be momentarily satisfying, but what's its business utility? I don't think there's any.

Rage doesn't pay the bills; being shrewd does.

---

82. PEOPLE WRITE CHEQUES

As an economy, we continue forging ahead into the era of electronic payment. Nevertheless, the grand ol' man of commercial compensation, the time-honoured cheque, is still alive'n'kicking. This is especially true for most SMEs. Will we all become Footsoldiers in the PayPal universe? I'm not convinced — although a better online mousetrap may still be in the offing and a younger generation of entrepreneurs and customers may prefer online payment as matter of course. So much of their personal lives are informed by online information, expression and culture. So why not invoices and payments?

Let me give you an example... Last year, I had to play hardball with a twenty-something website designer who refused to acknowledge "paper" in any form. He didn't even want his real-world address or phone number known/used. According to this techno-whippersnapper, "mail is so last-century." His world was online, he said. If I wanted to communicate with him, it had to be digital – only. I wanted to smack him, but I recognized that he was just a spokesman for his generation. I glimpsed the future in his spiel, and it was *not* good news for tomorrow's creditors.

Fortunately, 20th Century fuddy-duddyism isn't dead yet. The cheque-in-the-mail will remain the commercial method-of-choice for the foreseeable future. The cheque is a more personal payment medium than an electronic debit that rolls over automatically, month after month. Once approved, a recurring debit is mechanical. Cheque-writing, however, depends on human volition each time. Short of forcing a client to write a cheque at gunpoint, it's a voluntary activity that depends upon customer compliance. This explains its durability as the predominant payment style.

People authorize and execute cheques, and *people*, being mercurial, have to be dealt with skillfully. Sometimes sweetly, sometimes less so – but always with skill. Anytime a receivables manager takes action on slow-pay or no-pay, he or she has entered a world in which the quality of personal contact is paramount. Like successful selling, securing payment and guaranteeing customer retention require a healthy dose of personal poise. After all, what are we attempting to accomplish? We're "selling" a pastdue customer on the idea of voluntary payment.

---

83. A RINGSIDE SEAT

I'm going to return to the theme of barking, snarling and growling. Don't do it! Anyone calling for cash has to present appropriately, and that means professionally. Most customers bridle at the hectoring, bullying style of cash-recovery they associate (often wrongly) with collection. Nasty won't cut it. All you get is nasty in return. Or avoidance.

Suppliers require cash conversations that go as smoothly as possible and achieve the desired results. What they don't need are unnecessary collisions and busted relationships. Finding the right touch, and the person who's got it, is a constant challenge in receivables work. In the chapter on customer intimacy, I suggested this breezy formula: "firm but friendly." Sometimes we have to be a little more of one than the other, depending upon the demands of the situation. But as a general rule for how we behave, this is the right combination. Strong people-skills and a commitment to customer care have to be present in all departments of every business, but they're especially prized in Accounts

Receivable where those impromptu cash chats can turn very sour very quickly.

Money is a funny thing. Discussions about cash can get ugly, bringing out the worst in human nature. They don't call it "filthy lucre" for nothing! And unfortunately, there are way too many unskilled cash-cops who believe that the best way to communicate with garden-variety slow-payers is to bellow, threaten and humiliate. That kind of thinking is misguided, outmoded and its methods are unproductive. Do we need to scoop pastdue cash? Sure, we do. And yes, bad customers plague us all; they're the gophers in the garden of commerce. But if things are doomed to turn edgy and a little noisy, let it be because a debtor's scrappy attitude has made it unavoidable, not because it's your company's policy to flex its A/R biceps admiringly in the mirror.

Receivables-mining is a careful, methodical trade. You're mining for diamonds; your customer base is your diamond mine. You've worked hard to build the mine, and you need to manage it wisely if you want to continue extracting riches. Skill and experience in the A/R chair have a lot to do with it, but so does good old-fashioned horse-sense and being a people-person. Sure, some customers are tempted to manage their cash flow by disadvantaging yours, and they yield to that enticement regularly, but most residents of your client list are honest, hard-working diamond miners just like you. When these companies are in arrears, when they try to cut your corners, you can't sit on your hands.

That's a given. But you also don't have to lace on your boxing gloves and start throwing punches right away. I'll say it one last time:

Firm-but-friendly takes the laurels at ringside.

Prove your company places a value on customer relations. Put the boxing gloves away until there's a real reason to fight and a proven opponent to send sprawling to the mat.

---

84. ON THE FINAL FRONTIER OF CUSTOMER SERVICE

Some months ago, I received this email from a perplexed sales manager:

"We have a good customer who's suddenly stopped paying. We've never had a minute's trouble with this client before, and the street says the business is as solid as ever. The owner of our company has been calling the owner of the client company for days and his calls aren't being returned. So what's going on here? Is this a collection agency thing? Do I need to make that call?"

Let me dispense with the last two questions right away:

"Dear Mr. Sales Manager, put down the phone, please.

This is not a collection situation — at least, not yet.
Something's gone wrong, yes, but right now, you're
flying blind. You can't make good assumptions
or reliable decisions in an information vacuum.
More discovery needed."

While this situation is confusing if you're on the confused end of it, there may be a good reason why a dependable client with a pastdue invoice doesn't return executive calls. Panic reactions, like hurrying a good account into collection, won't help sort things out, and it's almost certain to make matters worse. When a headscratcher like this one comes out of left field, chances are there's a piece of the puzzle you haven't found yet. Could there be something else at issue? Very likely. And until you know what that "something" is, you can't and you shouldn't take decisive action.

Act in haste, repent at leisure.

With apologies to Capt. James Tiberius Kirk of the USS Enterprise…

Receivables management is the final frontier of customer
relations. The last member of your staff to communicate
with a valued client before he jumps ship is likely to be
your receivables manager.

Although customer intimacy isn't the first thing suppliers think of when they consider the duties of an A/R manager, savvy receivables supervision actually gives vendors a special opportunity to "touch" their customers and take a pulse. It may seem contradictory, but pastdue pursuit can be revealing. It can teach you many things worth knowing about your clients' problems, their objectives and the ways that your company can become a preferred supplier.

You should also be ready and willing to learn about customer problems *with* your company. That's not usually what a supplier wants to hear, but hearing it is still compulsory. Believe me, it's commercial gold when you do. Customer complaints allow suppliers to up the quality of their game and become more competent providers of goods and services. Problems you know about are problems you can fix, but the ones that go unrecognized silently kill customer confidence and bury repeat business.

As we've seen in this final section on receivables practice, non-paying clients can turn out to be unhappy clients, not just chickenizers, lame ducks or poverty-stricken cripples. And while customers brandishing a beef are as likely to be wrong as right, they always need to be taken seriously – that is, unless they're known to be tactical whiners or bazaaris who use hothoused disputes to buy time or squeeze price changes after-the-fact. During the course of routine conversation, your receivables staffer may hear about silent and unidentified shortcomings in your company's performance – shortcomings that are impacting negatively on your brand and compromising your profitability. Perhaps your delivery competence isn't what you think it is. Perhaps your invoices aren't getting out the door on time. Maybe your quality control people have dropped the ball once too often. And that's just a sampling. Believe me, there's more. But take the point, please...

Communication – even when it's criticism –
is the freeway to better business.

Anytime suppliers talk to clients, regardless of context, good things can ensue. When I'm on the job, I don't want customers freezing me out. I have questions; I want answers. To pose those questions and receive the "right" answers, I need a forum for discussion. The client has to do its part to provide that forum, and I have to do mine. A two-way street. That's why I believe an unhappy customer who's harbouring a dispute in silence is in the wrong. That client owes the vendor a frank and voluntary grumble. An unexplained refusal to pay an invoice demonstrates bad faith; it doesn't tell the whole story when there's a whole tale to be told. Suppliers don't read minds. As a responsible receivables manager, I want to receive direct, forthright complaints. I want unhappy customers to trust me to be an honest broker and give me a chance to provide effective customer service by making sure that grievances find their way to the right desk in the shortest possible time. Which brings me back to the sales manager with the collection query...

If your company is facing a similar problem – a

once-predictable client that abruptly stops paying *and* talking – before you pounce, take a deep breath. Perform a quick review of the papertrail: the contract or deal memo, ancillary notes, delivery sign-off and the billing. If everything checks out, if you feel your company has done what it was supposed to do from the point-of-sale to the point-of-delivery, you'll want your receivables manager to investigate further. What's the first thing you'll ask him to find out?

Has the non-paying client logged the unpaid invoice in its payables system? And is it scheduled for payment?

Your customer's A/P clerk will be the best first-level informant. She's the go-to staffer because she's in the best position to provide accurate payment information. Let's suppose, however, that you learn that the unpaid invoice was received long ago but never logged as a payable. It's languishing – unapproved and consigned to limbo – in someone's in-basket. Or perhaps you're told that it's *technically* approved but *politically stalled*. The inference you should take? Someone's sitting on the process. Now why would that be? And who's the party-pooper? Your A/P informant may spill the beans or just toss a few breadcrumbs for you to follow. Either way, you can infer with a fair degree of certainty that your once-happy customer is now discontented. And if it's not about the money or your product or service, it's about something else. But what? Until that's dragged to the surface, examined and resolved, your hands are tied. You can't get paid.

This is exactly how I discovered, some years ago, that the company I was working for had a severe but undiagnosed customer relations predicament. A long-time customer had turned off the money tap. Out of the blue. After weeks of effort on my part, which was met with complete silence on theirs, the client's controller finally checked-in. And were we in for a nasty shock when he did! What was all the "quiet" about? Apparently, one of our salesmen had made a "pass" at their young receptionist during a routine sales call. Mistake #1.

Did I say "young"? Try "underage"! A 16 year-old high school student temping during summer vacation. And it gets worse! Mistake #2? She was the owner's niece! Uh-boy. Well, no wonder Uncle Business Owner was furious. He simply refused to pay. That's how he expressed his fury. And he wanted satisfaction. Not hard to understand. His wife – the girl's aunt – was very, very upset. But here's the confound... For a guy so eager for some kind of immediate redress, he refused to tell us what his problem was. Not paying makes some sense. I get it. But not communicating for months? Not returning numerous calls and emails crying out for communication and context? That's just illogical. How could we possibly fix his wagon if we didn't know how the wheels had fallen off? He left us completely in the dark. And why was that? Because, he said later, he didn't think he could control his temper during a phone call. He was *that* angry – and afraid of the consequences of letting his anger loose! Go figure.

85. MAKE IT RIGHT – AND MAKE IT SOON!

There are 8 million stories in the Naked City – and most of them are cash-bearing. So, when a customer howls in the night, and the howl is justified, it makes no difference whether or not the howler's account is pastdue. There's a tree down; the road to payment is blocked. Gotta schlep that trunk out of the way. If you don't, the Brinks truck never gets through.

It's just human nature to try to evade icky, sticky moments. They hurt the head – notably when you're the one at fault. But there's no point in adding supplier avoidance to an already vexed scenario. In the vernacular of 2012: "Man-up!" When a dispute hits your doorstep, it has to be dealt with.

Face it and fix it. Make it right. And the sooner the better.

Being the diligent manager she is, your receivables supervisor has just placed a dispute memo on your desk. She's given you all the facts you need to know – facts pertaining to the invoice, the product or service the invoice represents and, above all, a clear account of the customer's "beef" in all its gory detail. And she's given you a timeline, too. She's told the complainant that she'll have a response within 48 hours (and preferably less). She's done her part and she's done it well. She's given you a "save" opportunity, and it's a timely one. Her conversation with that dissatisfied client is only one hour old. Fresh meat!

A valued customer with a realistic dispute deserves immediate attention and a timely corrective. Legitimate complaints are not hard to validate and they're not hard to satisfy. Moreover, showing your valued customer that you care about the after-market opinions of your clients – and your company's good name – with a rapid process of rectification can save a relationship that's been put in jeopardy by error or non-performance. They say it takes a big person to admit his/her errors. That's as true in business as it is at home. A swift commitment to service repair or reshipment of product, the application of a credit note or turning the offending invoice into a freebie, even contacting the customer in person or in print with a brief but unequivocal apology – these are the saving graces that reshape a potential divorce into a renewed and re-strengthened bond.

No supplier ever went bankrupt practising
the fine art of the sincere apology.

Nothing proves a supplier's dedication to product, service and customer satisfaction better than hearing the howl of unhappiness and doing something substantive about it a.s.a.p. This round may be lost, but you still have to keep your head in the larger game. The resilience of the relationship can be restored, and when it is, "our valued customer" will not be just rote, empty jargon. Your customer will *feel* valued. You'll have done "the right thing," and you'll have done it gracefully and without hesitation. Negative worth-of-mouth will be snuffed, and the highway will be clear for future business.

POSTSCRIPT

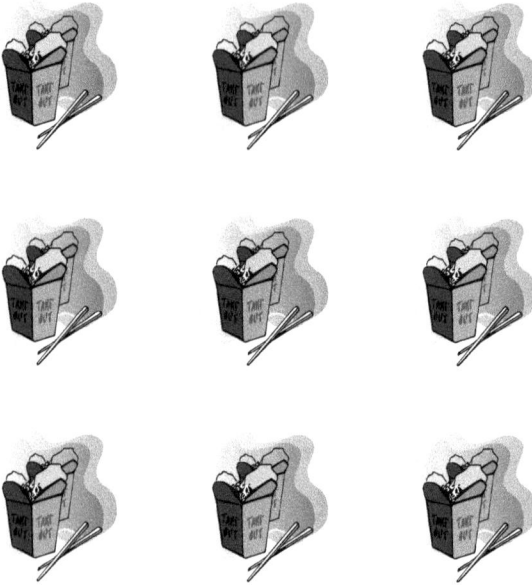

86. NINE TAKEAWAYS

One of the beauties of being human is the capacity to learn. Even when we don't realize it consciously, we're always sifting through the data of our experience and tweaking the process as we go. We're learning machines. We manage change. We do it in our personal lives, and we do it in our business lives, too. We upgrade. We improve. We aim for higher ground.

WHERE'S MY CASH?! is a fruit tree. It's the tree of my experience bearing the fruits of my expertise. My aim is true – at least, I hope so. And so I also hope you've found your share of receivables management education in these pages. If you've learned new strategies and attitudes that dismantle roadblocks to receivables competence, if they empower you to do business smarter and more profitably in future, then I've done my part. My objectives have been achieved: best practices shared. I'm content.

As I've demonstrated in this unpacking of theory and practice, non-existent or unskilled A/R management opens the door to cash-crunch, credit-crunch and bad debt. Receivables *mis*management is always a pain-producer. But as you've seen for yourself, it really doesn't have to be that way. Receivables distress and payment failure are mainly self-inflicted injuries. So take this closing opportunity to begin making inroads on improved cash-recovery. Make these 9 simple promises to yourself and your company. You won't be sorry you did.

Now, repeat after me:

1. **"We will install effective, systematic A/R management captained by a capable receivables manager."**

2. **"We will keep 'good paper,' because a thorough contractual papertrail is a pathway to profit."**

3. "We will develop and enforce firm but realistic credit management strategies, including best efforts at due diligence."

4. "We will remember that providing supply and service is an expense, making non-paying customers a cash liability."

5. "We will develop appropriate pastdue policies and procedures, policing all unpaid invoices decisively and professionally."

6. "We will not live in fear of or be bullied by troublesome, rude and obstinate customers, especially ones that owe us money. Bad clients are no longer welcome on our customer list."

7. "We will make every effort to negotiate reasonable payment arrangements with cooperative, valued customers, because good customers are golden."

8. "We will engage the services of a reputable collection agency or paralegal to help us defend the receivables we're unable to recover in-house."

9. "We will face all genuine customer disputes in the spirit of honesty, humility and gratitude, putting right what needs to be put right as quickly as possible."

Needless to say, these vows are not the be-all-and-end-all of top-shelf receivables security. But paying close attention to these articles of business faith will help put you on the right road to achieving a cash-conscious, profit-protecting, whole-business enterprise.

Look after your receivables, *Amigos and Amigas*, and I guarantee they'll look after you!

In the world of business books, it's not often you see
one about accounts receivable. Stu Woolley takes us on
a journey through the ways and means of maintaining
relationships with clients while ensuring payment. His
anecdotes about "chasing the weasel" and dealing with
the "chickenizers" are part of a step-by-step account of
avoiding the "fear of not getting paid" and the doomed
voyage of small claims court. WHERE'S MY CASH?! is
a cautionary tale for any business that delivers a service
or a product first and waits in limbo for payments that
may never arrive.

Scott Peterson
Business Host
CBC News Network
Toronto, ON

WHERE'S MY CASH?! should be required reading
for business school graduates and entrepreneurs alike.
Filled with practical, easy to follow tips from a long-
time accounts receivable practitioner, this book offers
an enjoyable read while unpacking the all-important
tasks in effectively managing receivables and
maximizing cash flow.

John Moore
Professor of Accounting,
Queen's School of Business
Queen's University, Kingston, ON

I've had the opportunity to start four companies. Each time, we managed to lay in all our fixed expenses: rent, payroll, equipment – long before we saw a dollar of revenue and even longer before we saw the first actual cheque arrive. Pro-forma balance sheets, income statements all fade into the background and one's focus is entirely on cash. Cash in, cash out; this is the lexicon of the entrepreneur. WHERE'S MY CASH?! is the primer you need to nurture and utilize this critical resource.

Paul K. Bates, FCMA, CMA, CMC.
Fellow, Society of Management Accountants of Canada
Certified Management Consultant
Special Advisor to the President, McMaster University;
DeGroote School of Business Executive Education.

If the question "where's my cash?" occupies your mind because it's having a negative impact on your business, then you're now holding the right guide to best cash practices. As Stu Woolley points out, it's time to rethink the whole approach to receivables, set priorities right and put a plan into action. Get out a highlighter and key-point your way to a workable A/R program.

Rick Wilks
Annick Press

When I agreed to preview WHERE'S MY CASH?!, I scarcely anticipated the exuberance of the writing, let alone so many thoughtful insights into how human nature confounds our best intentions to manage risk, receivables and cash flow effectively. Stu Woolley is a great champion for becoming cash conscious, and this book is a bracing refresher, blending practical tips born of long experience with the philosophy of a coach.

Robert A. Wood
President & CEO,
8020Info Inc.

In any business, your chief assets are money and time, especially the time of your talented staff. If you're spending endless employee hours trying to collect from overdue customers, then those hours aren't being spent growing your business. If you're also having operating funds challenges, then you need a better system for managing receivables and cash flow. WHERE'S MY CASH?! cuts to the heart of the issues that can keep you awake at night and shows you how to get your A/R under control and improve profit.

Phil Hood
President, Enter Music Publishing, Inc.
Publisher, DRUM!

WHERE'S MY CASH?! is a must-read for every owner or manager of a small to medium sized business. It clearly identifies why lack of cash is the critical factor that limits the growth of these companies and highlights how that same lack of cash is the main reason for failure. In addition, Stu Woolley describes organizational and operational fixes that will turn accounts receivable into cash. This is an easy read that will deliver measurable benefits to your organization.

Bob Pritchard
Marketing Consultant

A must-read for any business owner who wants to get paid! WHERE'S MY CASH?! explains how to manage receivables in a systematic, practical way. Stu Woolley's writing style is easy-to-read, educational and entertaining. Apply his advice and the cash will start to flow.

Mark Hanley
Enterprise Facilitator
KEDCO

Stu Woolley was born in the UK and grew up in Montreal when it was still Canada's premiere city. Following BA and MA degrees from McGill University, plus a long foray into the creative life as a songwriter, scriptwriter and writer of magazine articles, Stu has spent the past 20 years as an expert in accounts receivable management in Toronto, Vancouver and, most recently, eastern Ontario.

Nothing educates like practice, so WHERE'S MY CASH?!: TESTIMONY OF A MONEY-CHASER is a practitioner's distillation of two decades spent in the trenches of commercial receivables. As practice-driven business education, WHERE'S MY CASH?! is committed to the proposition that every business that invoices its customers can achieve effective cash-recovery.

In addition to operating Effective Receivables, an A/R management and consulting firm that helps businesses get paid, Stu continues to be musically engaged, as well as a serial scribbler in various formats. In addition, he's an almost daily visitor to the racquetball courts at Queen's University in Kingston.

Stu is married to Queen's education professor Lesly Wade-Woolley. Extending the family's academic traditions, their daughter Eve also attends McGill, and all three Woolleys are famously devoted to their American Field Goldens, Susie and Darla.

Find Stu Woolley at **www.effectivereceivables.com**